THROUGH THEIR EYES

A WINDOW TO OTHER SOULS

Edited By Lynsey Evans

First published in Great Britain in 2024 by:

Young Writers
Remus House
Coltsfoot Drive
Peterborough
PE2 9BF
Telephone: 01733 890066
Website: www.youngwriters.co.uk

All Rights Reserved
Book Design by Ashley Janson
© Copyright Contributors 2024
Softback ISBN 978-1-83565-544-3
Printed and bound in the UK by BookPrintingUK
Website: www.bookprintinguk.com
YB0594AZ

FOREWORD

Since 1991, here at Young Writers we have celebrated the awesome power of creative writing, especially in young adults, where it can serve as a vital method of expressing strong (and sometimes difficult) emotions, a conduit to develop empathy, and a safe, non-judgemental place to explore one's own place in the world. With every poem we see the effort and thought that each pupil published in this book has put into their work and by creating this anthology we hope to encourage them further with the ultimate goal of sparking a life-long love of writing.

Through Their Eyes challenged young writers to open their minds and pen bold, powerful poems from the points-of-view of any person or concept they could imagine – from celebrities and politicians to animals and inanimate objects, or even just to give us a glimpse of the world as they experience it. The result is this fierce collection of poetry that by turns questions injustice, imagines the innermost thoughts of influential figures or simply has fun.

The nature of the topic means that contentious or controversial figures may have been chosen as the narrators, and as such some poems may contain views or thoughts that, although may represent those of the person being written about, by no means reflect the opinions or feelings of either the author or us here at Young Writers.

We encourage young writers to express themselves and address subjects that matter to them, which sometimes means writing about sensitive or difficult topics. If you have been affected by any issues raised in this book, details on where to find help can be found at *www.youngwriters.co.uk/info/other/contact-lines*

CONTENTS

Byrchall High School, Ashton-In-Makerfield

Evie L (12)	1
Matas N (12)	2
Thomas Jennings (12)	4
Cosmo Law (11)	5
James D (11)	6
Noah Lavery (13)	7
Daniel Lavin (12)	8

Chase House School, Brownhills

Tamzin Sibson (15)	9

Claires Court School, Maidenhead

Dexter Barnard (13)	11
Matthieu Moorhouse (13)	12
Henry Eyton-Jones (13)	13
Seb Storey (14)	14
Ollie Credland	15
Tom Hickson (14)	16
Sam Buckley Souki (12)	17
Danial Tabbakh (12)	18
Gus Smith (13)	19
Michael Catchpole	20
Harry Mansfield (13)	21
James Letchford (14)	22
Peter Abraham-Leckie (14)	23
Trey Scott	24

Ercall Wood Academy, Telford

Rama Saladdin (14)	25

Inspire Education Group, Peterborough

Amogelang Selepe (18)	31

John Hampden Grammar School, Marlow Hill

Sam Morton (12)	33

Langley Park School For Girls, Beckenham

Ava McDonald (13)	35
Lucy Clarke	37

North Bridge House Canonbury, Islington

Finn Poulson	39
Fabio Lodolo	40

Queen's College, Taunton

Eleanor Rendall (15)	41

Red Balloon Worthing, Worthing

Ruby I	42

The Academy Of St Nicholas, Liverpool

Bietial Solomon (13)	43
Ema Ago (12)	44
Raven Scholes (14)	46
Chloe Tam (12)	48
Ayhan Battal (11)	50

Name	Page
Connor Moore (12)	52
Evelyn Wild (11)	54
O Moore (14)	55
Skye Ainsworth (14)	56
Savannah-Rose Rawlings-Baig (11)	58
Sonya Balkandzhievo (13)	59
Mymoona Al-Zoubi (12)	60
Ilana Herd (12)	62
Naina Aggarwal (13)	64
Sathyadharmaraj Shyam (14)	66
Anya Lock (12) & Annette Riley (13)	67
Matt Johnson (13)	68
Annice Damulina (13)	69
Amelia Brennan-Cullingford (12)	70
Ruby Barnabas (12)	71
Tallulah Rasmussen (11)	72
Serah Maria Anson (12)	73
Shalom Joseph (11)	74
Marco Meloro (11)	75
Ying Ki Yanki Chow (12)	76
Lily-Sue Shields (11)	77
Louise Garvey (12)	78
Isla Atkinson-Pye (13)	79
Lorena Soares (13)	80
Delilah Williams (12)	81
Moise Bwaka (12)	82
Aiham Halloudi (12)	83
Jessica Alvers (13)	84
Aniela Dominte (12)	85
Yan Situ (11)	86
Man Chun June Tsoi (12)	87
Alyssa Mercer (14)	88
Raseal Alser (11)	89
Nojus Akelaitis (11)	90
Kacper Dobranski (12)	91
Louis Fell (12)	92
Liam Johnson (12)	93
Thrina Datta (14)	94
Samanta Garklava (13)	95
James Ahmed (12)	96
Jolie Guano (13)	97
Poppy Wild (11)	98
Evie Killen (12)	99
Paulie Conroy	100
Oluwaferanmi Kolawole (11)	101
Evan Kelly (13)	102
Saja Harrud (12)	103
Refat Muyedinov (13)	104
Talia Elmahdi (13)	105
Lillie-May Wong-Morgan (12)	106
Harley Magee (11)	107
Michael Kanoniuk (13)	108
Frankee Perry (11)	109
Aseel Alser (11)	110
Toluwanimi Kolawole (14)	111
Usra Siddiqui (13)	112
Yasrib Siddiqui (12)	113
Briana Silva (12)	114
Giancarlo Pili (12)	115
Leighton Yates (12)	116
Madeleine Wileman-Duckworth (13)	117
Hannah Majewska (13)	118
Seren Egan (12)	119
Mollie Haresnape (14)	120
Darcie Corser (13)	121
Jan Abdu (11)	122
Csenge Kishonti (13)	123
Ishita Chowdhury (12)	124
Jessica Kaufman (13)	125
Sam William Liddell (13)	126
Maegan Never (12)	127
Charlotte Hon (13)	128
Phoebe Child (11)	129
Finlee Perry (13)	130
Sam Hughes (12)	131
Luna Pacheco (13)	132
Maria Ragone Lopes (11)	133
Omran Alhussein (11)	134
Darcy Bate (12)	135
Matilda Kalita (11)	136
Nevin Kulangara Sabu (12)	137
Berat Coskuncay	138
Giovanna Mileo (13)	139
Jessica Bennett (13)	140

Arjin Ali (13)	141
Corey	142
Aisha Abdillahi (12)	143
Hollie Winterson (13)	144
Jazmin Atkinson (12)	145
Joseph Myles (11)	146
Heidi Fane (12)	147
Angel Moyo (12)	148
Heidi Harrison (12)	149
Kasra Gohari (13)	150
Adam Formby (12)	151
Amelia Gaines (11)	152
Scott Pye (13)	153
Amelia Wells Roberts (12)	154
Bobby Blyth (11)	155
Demi Parker (12)	156
Josh Feeley (13)	157
Alaa Emziane (12)	158
Mustafa Mahmood (12)	159
Max Mercer (12)	160
Daniel Kidd (13)	161

William Bussey (14)	180
Cameron Lewis (13)	181
George Coates (14)	182
Mia Barwick (14)	183
Molly Byrne-Smith (14)	184
Elsie Kalaker (14)	185

The Hammond School, Chester

Marisa Becker (13)	162
Clara Hayward (12)	163
Felicity Gray-Shaw (12)	164
Harriet Maughan (12)	165
Christie Morgan (12)	166
Catherine Hampson (12)	167

Trinity High School, Redditch

Bethany Pearson (13)	168
Kaiden Collins-Evans (13)	170
Oliver Cureton-Phillips (14)	171
Ashton Hands (13)	172
Evie Hawkins (14)	173
Falak Aziz (14)	174
Millie Jones (13)	175
Ayaan Hussain (14)	176
Izzy Louth (14)	177
Kye McEntee (13)	178
Henry Power (13)	179

THE POEMS

The Love For My Brother

My little brother is the best person to exist,
No he really is, I insist,
I love him, that's for sure,
He's caring, kind, passionate and more,
He has Down syndrome, he's really cute,
And he walks around in his dinosaur suit,
Even though he might be judged,
When he kisses me, my make-up is smudged,
I guide him on a path when he feels alone,
And when he's upset we sing 'Into the Unknown',
His smile lights up the room,
Even when it's doom and gloom,
He makes us laugh, that's no doubt,
But he never knows what we're laughing about,
And so what if he has an extra chromosome?
He's just like us, down to the bone,
And people need to understand,
That he can do anything on command,
When he comes into my room with my mother,
That's when I know that there is another
Day spent with my little brother.

Evie L (12)
Byrchall High School, Ashton-In-Makerfield

Open Your Eyes

Open your eyes,
Keep them open as you don't know who fought for you.
Open your eyes,
Trenches used as helpful benches just to invade.
Open your eyes,
Blood, mud and dirt splattered around the soil, acting as fertiliser.
Open your eyes,
You stand on the world that was changed more than you.
Open your eyes,
Was the bloodshed not worth it for us to remember?
Open your eyes,
Poppies saved us, a flower, which brought us together.
Open your eyes,
Nights wasted, lack of sleep because of the enemies.
Open your eyes,
Don't forget the reason they fought for you.
Open your eyes,
Criminals, immigrants, untrained civilians are the people inside.
Open your eyes,
Blood, mud and dirty all lost because of war.
Open your eyes and remember them,
Just don't forget their souls are watching you.
Open your eyes,
They will never come back, their death has been fought for.

Open your eyes,
They still fight even in death.

Matas N (12)
Byrchall High School, Ashton-In-Makerfield

A Truly British Day

Double-decker buses roll down the streets,
With houses in rows, so little and neat.
Flags are draped over the windows with care,
To put on display their Great British flair.
For on this great day, something would happen,
That 'thing' would have tea, crumpets and passion.
Get to the river to find the best place,
Lay out the picnic, let's watch the boat race!
It's close, it's tight as they race round the bends,
They're on the home straight! It's nearly the end!
The boats cross the line, the Cambridge crew win!
It's time for a pint, let's get to The Inn!
Karaoke's on, we all start to sing,
A truly British day, God save the King!

Thomas Jennings (12)
Byrchall High School, Ashton-In-Makerfield

Eyes In The War

Running and hiding
Shooting and shielding
Advancing and retreating
Yeah, that's what's going on in the war.

Many dying and suffering
With no one to help but yourself
Relying on the slimmest ray of hope
Yeah, that's what's going on in the war.

Buildings shattered and blown up
People trapped under rubble
Left to rot and
Yeah, that's what's going on in the war.

Flying and escaping in the skies
Chased by enemies and shot down
Set ablaze and forced to leave your loved ones
Yeah, that's what's going on in the war.

Cosmo Law (11)
Byrchall High School, Ashton-In-Makerfield

Untitled

My name is James,
I have lots of friends,
I love to play games,
The fun never ends.

In my home, I'm not alone,
It's not just people in my house,
I'm surrounded by three caring sisters,
Who are home,
We've got a gecko who likes to eat a louse.

I'm lucky to have many friends,
They are kind, generous and funny,
Back in April, I travelled to France,
Where I studied the Eiffel Tower,
My friends gave me money,
I have got lots of power.

In school,
I made a few,
My friends call me a fool,
They're all new.

James D (11)
Byrchall High School, Ashton-In-Makerfield

WWII Soldier

Bang! Argh! Help!
Terrorising isn't it? These are the sounds of war.
Not all jolly is it? But important isn't it?
The backbone of giving you a happy, safe world.
And we battle so you can become who you are.
You must be the change for you to see a peaceful world.

Noah Lavery (13)
Byrchall High School, Ashton-In-Makerfield

Penguin

P erilous against the snow
E xtreme speed in the freezing cold sea
N utritious fish for lunch, tasty!
G liding fearlessly across the ice
U sing their flippers to gain speed
I ntelligent to catch fish
N ow bonding with the snow.

Daniel Lavin (12)
Byrchall High School, Ashton-In-Makerfield

Chicken Named Teriyaki

It was a dark day for all of us on the farm
We woke one morning to sure alarm
To my dear dad, bones being eaten
Now I'm all alone in Nuneaton.
I had to escape, I had to break free
Had to break loose from captivity
I left my family, now I'm all alone
They're back on the farm in Atherstone.
A little old lady picked me up
And shoved me into the back of a pickup truck
I was lone, alone, bruised and beaten
Now I was chicken-napped on the way to Nuneaton.
I had to find a way to get away today
There had to be a way.
The truck hit a bump in the middle of the road
The old woman screamed like the croak of a toad
The boot flew open and my cage fell out
I was stranded again on the side of a roundabout.
Which way should I go
To get to a place better than my home?
I went on my way and took the next right
Then a family of rats gave me a fright
They introduced themselves, very formal for a rat
"Our names are Pedro, Sam, Sophie and Nat."
Nat told me of a safehouse for lost chickens like me
And they gave me a nickname, they called me Teriyaki.

So, off I go, to the safehouse, I flee
I follow along Main Street until I get to KFC
When I step inside, the horror it brings
My friends are in burgers, legs and wings
I'm a scared little chicken who's surely in for it
My story ends here, at the bottom of this bucket.

Tamzin Sibson (15)
Chase House School, Brownhills

Same Class, Parallel Views

Silly children messing about
I've given so many detentions - I have lost count
The class is aroused, a student is on the desk dancing around
Shouting and laughter start to get loud
Get me out, get me out, get me out!

I'm trying to teach them, they won't work
Then one of the boys starts to smirk
I brace myself, expecting the worst
Pens fly everywhere, the class goes berserk
I feel it inside me, I can hear the shout
Get me out, get me out, get me out!

Boring old teachers, blocking the sun
No running in the halls, they have banned all the fun
Three hours of homework waiting to be done
I am forced to do it by my strict, annoying mum
I have to study until she's pleased
Let me leave, let me leave, let me leave!

Nine hours of hell, I'm feeling unwell
I go to the nurse but she sends me back
My frustration and anger starting to attack
When I get back, I drift off and nap
I wake up and move my body, with a great heave
Let me leave, let me leave, let me leave!

Dexter Barnard (13)
Claires Court School, Maidenhead

Cyclops' Breeze

My vessel built with love and passion
As I gently sail on the lake of dreams
Navigating through live's turbulent streams.

He took my blue electric cover off me
My eyes finally seeing the glorious sun
Clip after clip, rope after rope
My sail flapped out with joy!

I hit the water
The sensation of the cold shivered my plastic shell
Then I was off
Open to the ocean
I felt so free as never before at that moment
The delicate sun kissed my deck with golden light.

My body was drowning in the water
Would I ever survive this cold shivering substance?
The wind caught my pale green sail.

It caught it too much
I was panicking
So my driver too.

Matthieu Moorhouse (13)
Claires Court School, Maidenhead

Your Worst Nightmare

Waking up every morning,
Not wanting to wake up,
Being cold all night,
Being hungry and thirsty,
Not being clean and happy,
Everyone's worst nightmare!

Not having any money,
Not having any family or friends,
The only thing you own is yourself
And your clothes,
Everyone's worst nightmare!

Feeling unloved,
Not being cared for,
Feeling sick inside your stomach,
Depending on other people's kindness,
Everyone's worst nightmare!

Not even eating a full meal,
Going to sleep hungry,
People staring at you like you're an animal,
Everyone's worst nightmare!

What would you do?

Henry Eyton-Jones (13)
Claires Court School, Maidenhead

Fed-Ex Delivery

Every time I look around, I see a white abyss.
Crisp air;
Cutting through.

I hear the shutters shoot up.
The burn of rubber cuts the smell out my nose
As I lift the product, my sweat lands into my mouth
Salty.

The splinter slides through the layers of my skin
Layer one;
A tickle
Layer two;
Pain forming
Layer three;
Downright, agony.

As I shake the driver's hand,
I notice the texture of his hand.
Dust.
Like he's just left a rugby pitch,
This fact is hard to circumvent
As this man is trying to lacerate my hand right off
Rip.
Rip.
Rip...

Seb Storey (14)
Claires Court School, Maidenhead

The Crash

When my tyres reach a
Dirt track, my heavy suspension
Leans down onto my aluminium core.

The heavy body sitting
on my saddle, putting all of
His pressure on my carbon
Frame, waiting for the rider to
Make a mistake.

As we approach the high ramp
We brake in a panic and fall down
The 20-foot drop between both of the ramps.

With a half split core, the rider
Looks in disbelief at the
Deformed pedals and the near
Flat, torn tyres.

The rider looks for help
With his broken leg, the ambulance
Come and clear up his mess.

Ollie Credland
Claires Court School, Maidenhead

Owen Farrell

Back on the pitch again,
Going through all that pain.
It was quite a slow start,
Our line was starting to part.

Our opponents got one down,
That really made me frown.
Smith got through their line,
The forwards began to bind.

Back in our half,
Doesn't Marler look daft?
Been called off for 10...
Oh... we are winning again!

They're pushing for the win,
We're not letting them in!
The final whistle blows!
It's another day for the Rose!

Tom Hickson (14)
Claires Court School, Maidenhead

A Dog's Life

In the morning, when the owner drops off the son
I sneak into the sheep field opposite
Then I chase the sheep for ten minutes
I then hear the owner's car and hurry back into the house
I jump onto the son's bed like nothing happened
I hear the door open and I come rushing to the door.

Later in the evening, the owner goes to pick up the son
I go to his room and stay on his bed again
Now, for the second time, I hear the door open
I go rushing for the door to greet them both.

Sam Buckley Souki (12)
Claires Court School, Maidenhead

When Does It End?

When does it end?
No one knows,
How do we exist?

Many universes,
Many planets,
And on Planet Earth, we are
Fighting for ridiculous reasons.

When we are born,
Our parents name us
Without ourselves deciding it.
When does it end?

Well, no one knows
What will happen,
Even if everything
Turns to nothing,
There would still be a thing.

When does it end?

Danial Tabbakh (12)
Claires Court School, Maidenhead

Ukraine

The bombs are falling, people are crawling,
The missiles are firing, people are dying.

Swish, swish, boom, it has shattered the room,
We must leave, we must go,
For the Russians are coming and everything will blow.

I'm riding on a train,
Everything is plain,
Leaving my family - it's turning into fantasy.
I am going to a safe country to try and start a new life for me.

Gus Smith (13)
Claires Court School, Maidenhead

Through Their Eyes

I have never been so upset!
Because of that disgusting, racial threat,
And how much they should regret.

Their words can't hurt me,
They sure do sting.
All of their anger,
Because of the colour of my skin.

In unity we stand, a vibrant array,
Rejecting the darkness that racism may lay.
Diversity's beauty, a tapestry bright,
Ignites a world where all hearts unite.

Michael Catchpole
Claires Court School, Maidenhead

Pavel

The depressed and lonely soul
Caring but quiet
A doctor - but a servant.

A Jew, in a German environment
Like a fish on land
Or a bird in the ocean.

The small and fragile man
A person who once had feelings
Someone who longs for their family.

Lucky to be alive
But also unfortunate
Near the end and fading fast...

Harry Mansfield (13)
Claires Court School, Maidenhead

Through The Eyes Of A Jewish Prisoner

P eople I know disappear, every day
R etching smells come from the shower, every day
I have to do unpaid work, every day
S ome of the guards beat us, every day
O n the towers, we are watched, every day
N obody leaves, yet people arrive every day
E scape attempts fail, every day
R emember us, every day.

James Letchford (14)
Claires Court School, Maidenhead

Bruno's Mind

I wonder, I wonder
Who are those people?
Why do they wear the same clothes?

What's for breakfast?
Pavel should get some credit.
I wanna make another swing.
Why did we move here?

I wonder, I wonder...
House, breakfast, move, people.
What is Dad going to do?
I should go annoy Gretel.
When will Dad be home?

Peter Abraham-Leckie (14)
Claires Court School, Maidenhead

Pavel's Life

Pavel has gone through a lot in his life,
started as a doctor, ended up as a servant.
He's lost his family and friends and many more of his peers.
They were slaughtered and forced into a gas chamber, while
children were crying and begging for mercy.
So let us honour him for all his doings
and not giving up in times that were hard.

Trey Scott
Claires Court School, Maidenhead

The Doctor's Healing Symphony

I am back again for my long lucubrate nine hours of restless work.
Ready to put a brave, alleviated, fearless face on.
Ready for the unknown.
Ready to burn the midnight oil away.
The feelings of fear, sadness and anger
triggered by negative headlines.
Ready to leave me stuck in a pattern of frequent monitoring,
seeing the feeling of despair eradicate your patient's face.
Ready to burn the midnight oil away.
Time moving at snail's pace.
Where in a second, you can potentially be the hands that cure someone's
disease or illness or anything that could prompt their assistance.
Ready to take all the chances possible.
Ready for anything.

The dim-lit ER where shadows entwine,
as a writer, as a doctor
my pen, a scalpel on the parchment's page,
recording tales of life, both joy and rage.
Each patient, a protagonist in their plot,
their struggles and pain, interwoven within my narrative
the pulse of their stories, a heartbeat's verse,
in the ink's embrace, their pain dispersed.

Yet, in this script, some chapters end,
a writer-doctor, condolences to send.
Through tear-stained words, compassion bleeds,
on the paper's canvas, where empathy leads.
The ER's pages, a canvas of despair,
a writer-doctor, burdened by the wear.
In the quiet aftermath, when the night is done,
I pen the stories of battles lost and won.

Diagnosing medical conditions, a puzzle to unfold,
developing treatment plans, a personalised mould.
Prescribing medications, a precise remedy,
performing medical procedures, a skilled symphony.
Providing preventive care, a shield against strife,
educating patients, empowering with life.
Counselling with empathy, a tender embrace,
collaborating with teams, a synchronised race.
Documenting patient care, a meticulous trace,
keeping up with knowledge, a perpetual chase.
Overseeing operational duties, an organised pace,
advocating for patients, a steadfast grace.
Leading healthcare teams, a beacon of light,
participating in quality improvement, a commitment to right.
Researching and innovating, a quest for insight,
each responsibility a part of the doctor's plight.
In the solemn sanctuary of the ER's domain,
words of solace whispered void of disdain.

A writer-doctor, bearing witness to the lone,
in the tapestry of existence, compassion is sown.

To the family of the departed, I softly say,
"We did all we could, I'm sorry for your loss."
To the survivor clinging to hope's fragile thread,
"You're stronger than you know, keep fighting."
To the one facing their final moments with grace,
"You're not alone, we're here with you."
To the weary soul who finds solace in sleep,
"Rest now, your pain is over."
In the stillness of the ER's solemn space,
words of comfort uttered with grace.
A writer-doctor, bearing witness to life's end,
through sorrow and joy, a healer and friend.

To the soul who's all alone, in solitude's embrace,
where shadows linger, leaving little trace.
No hand to hold, no comforting word,
a writer-doctor, their presence assured.
In the hushed chamber where truth is laid bare,
amidst the silence, with hearts laid bare.
No one by their side in this moment of dread,
a writer-doctor, their sorrow to tread.
With empathy's touch and a heavy heart,
words of solace, a compassionate art.
In the silence of their solitude's reign,
a writer-doctor, their comfort to feign.

To the soul who's all alone, in dire need,
a writer-doctor, their sorrow to heed.
In the absence of companionship's grace,
a writer-doctor, their presence to embrace.

In the dim-lit room, shadows softly glide,
as a solemn sentinel, I stand beside.
The final moments draw near, a whispered sigh,
I am the last they'll see as they bid goodbye.
With tender hands, I offer solace and peace,
guiding them gently to life's final release.
Their eyes meet mine, a fleeting glance,
a silent exchange, a final dance.
In the quiet of the room, emotions entwine,
I bear witness to their life's final line.
As their journey ends, I hold their hand tight,
a beacon of comfort in the fading light.
In the stillness of the moment, time stands still,
a sacred bond forged, an indelible will.
I am the last they'll see, a comforting guide,
as they embark on their eternal tide.

Through tear-stained words, I must now tread,
for the news I bear weighs heavy as lead.
To my beloved, with trembling voice,
"I must share news that leaves no choice."
Your illness, a foe we hoped to fight,
but the battle ahead is shrouded in night.

With all my knowledge, all my skill,
the prognosis is bleak, and it breaks my will.
In the quiet of this hallowed space,
I hold you close, in our embrace.
Though my hands have healed many a soul,
this burden, my love, takes its toll.
Together, we'll face the uncertain road,
each step a heavy, weary load.
But know this, my dearest heart:
in this journey, we'll never be apart.
In the silence of the ER's domain,
love and sorrow intertwined, our refrain.
A writer-doctor, bearing weight of fate,
in the tapestry of love, we navigate.

To the soul facing the darkness alone,
"You're not forgotten, your presence is felt."
To the one whose solitude echoes in the room,
"Your strength in solitude is profound."
To the heart heavy with the weight of loneliness,
"Your story matters, even in the silence."
To the individual navigating life's solitary path,
"You're not alone, I'm here to walk beside you."
In the silent sanctuary of the Emergency Ward's domain,
words of solace whispered void of disdain.
A writer-doctor, bearing witness to the lone,
in the tapestry of existence, compassion is sown.

In the dim-lit ER, shadows cast their gloom,
I stand helpless, trapped within this room.
Despite my efforts, despite my skill,
I cannot ease the pain, cannot fulfil.
The weight of their suffering, heavy on my chest,
I offer solace, but it's not enough, at best.
My hands tremble, my heart aches with despair,
for I cannot mend what seems beyond repair.
I search for answers, for a glimmer of hope,
but sometimes, all I find is a slippery slope.
No matter how hard I try, how much I care,
I cannot change the outcome, cannot repair.
In the silence of the night, I silently weep,
for the ones I couldn't save, the promises I couldn't keep.
I carry their stories, their struggles, their pain,
a heavy burden, a haunting refrain.
In the dim-lit ER, I confront my defeat,
but still, I'll continue, with unwavering beat.
For though I cannot help every soul that I meet,
I'll stand by their side, in their journey, complete.

This is inspired by my dad, an emergency doctor, and my mom, who is both a doctor and an enthusiast of writing. It's also a tribute to my grandfather, who didn't have the chance to witness this accomplishment.

Rama Saladdin (14)
Ercall Wood Academy, Telford

Human Nature

I gape at them from afar
Far beyond the soaring mountains
Far beyond the ever-changing stars
Their diminutive minds cannot begin to fathom
Any creature more divine than themselves
They have tried to prove my existence
But to no avail, they concede defeat
I guess it's just human nature

I watch them grow from innocent little beings
To horrible monsters, the downfall of humanity
Their greed overshadows their morality
Swift and skilled with sharp knives
Behind the backs of their loved ones
Love is not synonymous to pain and suffering
Far too stubborn to ever learn
I guess it's just human nature

Their greedy hearts and selfish ways
They give only when they take
They cover for bloodstained hands
They never learn, history repeats once again
A story all too familiar, a vicious cycle
Stone-blind to what lies before them
Their world is crumbling and bleeding
I guess it's just human nature

Monsters of their own destruction, venomous tongues
To protect their own, they start wars
War against humanity, for the sake of humanity?
I guess it's human nature.

Amogelang Selepe (18)
Inspire Education Group, Peterborough

Archie The Dog: A Walk

My name is called,
Where are we going?
She says, "Come on, walkies."
Yes, it's walkies,
The people put on their coats,
My annoying leash is attached to my collar, and off we go!

The smells are all familiar,
The countryside air brushing against my fur,
The grain with that oaty-ness and the potatoes, potatoey,
The petrol of the tractors in the nearby fields,
The sights of the colourful fields and sky,
William, the horse, and the wrecked forest,
Everything is the same.

We enter a field,
My leash is taken off,
A snack as my reward,
I quickly scoff it down,
Before running free of my will.

This field seems endless,
It goes on forever,
But it doesn't matter,
I'm having fun running around, crazy,
Rolling around in fox poo,
Which my owners hate but I love,

Barking at infernal stones,
Behaving as mad puppies do
Despite my years of age.

After many fields, tirelessly running and barking,
We arrive back home where I can be lazy,
And ask for more snacks,
Then I lie in front of the fireplace,
Before dreaming of a world with no stones.

Sam Morton (12)
John Hampden Grammar School, Marlow Hill

My Only Friends Are Stars

I look up at the sky and wonder in desperation
If stars have emotions too,
If they feel despair and heartbreak.

Maybe the stars can see me crying
And feel the same emotions I feel now.
They twinkle softly
And I can't wipe away the tears on my cheeks.

And this is your fault as well, you know?
For putting my heart in my throat
And my brain in my shoes.
It's all because of you.

Your smile,
Your laugh.
The way you walk and talk,
The way you 'are'.

Your words cut like daggers
But your lips speak nothing but the truth.
Your eyes are warm and welcoming
Yet hold an ounce of integrity.

You're perfect in every way.
And that's why stars are my only friends,
As they cannot deceive nor hurt me
Like you do.

That's why I love the stars,
Because they cannot leave me
Like people do.

Ava McDonald (13)
Langley Park School For Girls, Beckenham

Frankenstein's Monster

Why was I left alone by society?
A perfect human being pieced together
With 'beautiful features',
But somehow I was not a man,
For I was a monster.
Because I was never born,
I was made under a scalpel and knife.
That was the start of my life.
I didn't know if this was normal or not,
Was I someone's son?
A son that was abandoned and forgotten.
Left alone by the world, an outcast.
A monster that didn't know the difference
Between the good and bad,
The light and dark.
What was wrong?
What was right?
A monster by day, a monster by night.
But who were the real monsters?
The ones that judge and fight?
Well, I tell you,
It's humankind.
They're the ones that kill,
Harming other people and making them ill,
Making society sick at their will.

Because monsters are created not in a lab,
Or studied in a book,
Instead, they are made,
An infection on a blank page.
I never wanted this,
I never wanted to be a 'monster'.
I wanted to be someone's son,
Someone's sweetheart,
But instead, all I got was hurt;
A stranger's heart
And a head pieced together by wiry thread.

Lucy Clarke
Langley Park School For Girls, Beckenham

Void Yet Divine

I can hear the rushing waters
Of the rivers running by
I can hear all the birds singing
Like robins and magpies.
All the deer are running around
The frosty green trees
All the flowers are slowly opening
For all the honeybees.
The moonlight glimmers
Through the trees
And the luscious green grass.
All the icicles on the bush
That almost mimics glass
The blank snow beneath my feet
Void yet divine.

Finn Poulson
North Bridge House Canonbury, Islington

Rosy Lips

With lips so red she sits alone
Her eyes set upon mine
And her lids dyed by her madness
Inside a cage hidden and unseen
She stays unknowing and unheard
A kiss she shares with a ghost
A reminder of her victims
No minions does she have
But those which love her
Just drones are left
Phantoms of past might.

Fabio Lodolo
North Bridge House Canonbury, Islington

Two Lines That'll Never Cross

Hope. A chance this time it'll all work out.
I look up to the sky to relieve my doubt,
But clutching this blue stick of potential,
I shiver knowing I'm missing something essential.
I turn it over, firstly look away.
Do I even want to see it anyway?

In a desperate prayer, I flip it around.
I blink and the dreaded tears fall down.
My hands can't hold it steady anymore,
So I let it go and jump as it falls to the floor.
And honestly, I find it hard to believe,
What sort of woman am I if I can't conceive?

Maybe I deserve this ache to procreate?
Maybe I did something to deserve this cruel fate?
I feel so small as I think of the opportunities missed,
The little face I know I'll never get to have kissed.
I bring my hands up to my teary face,
And hold myself in a cold embrace.
Why won't they let me be what I feel I should be?

Eleanor Rendall (15)
Queen's College, Taunton

Through The Eyes Of Desire

We think the same, feel the same, we are alike in all ways.
We are two beings connected through fate;
The strings of my being keep me chained to you.
I know each part of you, like you know each part of me.
Our love is suffocating, I cry and plead that I can't breathe,
I choke and trip with every word that exits your mouth.
Your love feels like a prison,
Your fists the bars that keep me glued and sealed.
Stuck.
You crawl into the den of my mind,
Inspecting each crevice
With a grip that pulls a string on my heart,
Each time you raise your hands.
I wish to be free; I desire an escape from it all.

Ruby T
Red Balloon Worthing, Worthing

I Am Deeply Grateful

I am grateful for having a life and a home.
I am grateful for the health I own.
I am grateful for having eyes that allow
Me to see the beautiful bright sunshine.
I am grateful for having the chance to
Always pray which gives me strength and guidance.

I am grateful for having family, that makes me
Feel powerful and confident hyping me up
And never giving up on me.
I am grateful for my friends for their
Help and support towards me.
I am grateful for my teachers who
Inspired me to gain more knowledge and be the best
Version of myself.
I am grateful for all the struggles and
Troubles that I faced
Because they are the reason why I am brave and ambitious
today.

Again, I am grateful for everything
I have in my life!

Dietiul Solomon (13)
The Academy Of St Nicholas, Liverpool

Silenced By Shadows

She walks with her head down low
Her voice barely a whisper, faint and slow
A shy introvert, she keeps to herself
Not seeking attention or yearning for wealth
But little do they know, the pain she hides
For she's the target of their cruel jibes
Bullied and belittled, day after day
It's like a nightmare she can't seem to shake away
They mock her for her quiet ways
Never understanding the price she pays
To be different, in a world so loud
She feels lost and small in a suffocating crowd
She dreams of standing up to those who tease
But her courage falters, her fear she can't appease
For she's been told she's just not enough
And it's hard to believe when that's all she's heard since she was young
Yet behind those shy eyes lies a heart of gold
That's been hardened and bruised but it still holds
The strength to rise despite the pain
To break free from the chains and start anew again
For she is more than just a shy introvert
She's a fighter, a survivor, no one can hurt
Her spirit may be gentle, but it's fierce and strong
And she'll prove all her bullies oh so wrong

So don't underestimate the quiet girl you see
For she's more than meets the eye, you'll soon come to see
She's brave and resilient, and she'll stand tall
For she's a shy introvert, but she's not weak at all.

Ema Ago (12)
The Academy Of St Nicholas, Liverpool

Your Darling, Helen Of Troy

Oh, my daring mother Leda, oh my darling sister Clytemnestra,
Do you hear my soft mutterings, my prayers,
Asking that I remain within your fondest memories as you do in mine?
Do you implore the gods to return me home before the last leaf falls?
Oh, my darling mother Leda, am I still your beautiful girl, even throughout my most foolish act?
Oh, my darling sister Clytemnestra, do you think about holding me in your arms again,
Am I still worthy of your affection?

Oh, my darling husband Menelaus, do I continue to fuel your passion even in my absence?
Would you forgive my disloyalty, my promiscuity if I apologised at your feet?
Will you then come with your soldiers, perhaps even with the almighty Aristos Achaion of Phthia in your wake?
Oh, my darling husband Menelaus, does the world still see me as the beautiful Helen of Sparta?

Oh, mighty Jove, son of Kronos, can you hear my silent pleas, my woeful sobs, my yearning for home?
Is my beguiling beauty not the result of your swan, of your thunderous power?
Or is it my own grandiosity that led me here?
Is that why you allow me to remain here longer, to repent for my wrongdoings?

Oh, mighty Jove, father of my half-god flesh, is the blood of this raging war upon my hands?
If so, send me a sign, a bolt of lightning, to give me the chance to change.
Your darling, Helen of Troy.

Raven Scholes (14)
The Academy Of St Nicholas, Liverpool

True Or False? Real Or Not Real?

Things are going down, I think I'm gonna drown.
Suffocating in the air, that's just the small things I've got to bear.
Everything is unknown, even in my own home.
All I feel is alone, things I think are so below.

The walls are crumbling, this is getting interesting.
Where life is getting harder, I can't seem to find my border.
Lost in the sea, where emptiness is all I can see.
Creatures surround me, is this who I want to be?

Now I'm trapped in a cage where there's no escape.
Where there are pretty landscapes
Always lie an unbreakable gate
Am I taking the bait?

Monsters are my friend,
So I don't need to defend.
Where believing is a weakness,
This world is leaving me speechless.

Losing all hope, I can't even cope.
Everything is now dead, I can't even breathe.
Please just let me leave, I can't even believe.
Then colours are grey, all I can do is pray.
But now I'm the prey, are you fazed?
Society's making me insane, no one here
Even has a brain.

I'm tired, I really am.
But all I can do is hold on and fight.
'Cause this, this is my life.

Chloe Tam (12)
The Academy Of St Nicholas, Liverpool

Inner Battles

In shadow's deep, a student's sigh,
Each day's battle, a weary cry.
Parents' demands, a heavy weight,
Their dreams imposed, a cruel fate.
Exhausted limbs and mind, a storm,
In endless loops, thoughts deform.
Overthinking, a relentless stream,
A tangled web, a haunting dream.
School's harsh glare, a constant test,
A battleground where souls are stressed.
Pressure mounts, like heavy chains,
Dragging down through endless plains.
In smiles worn thin, a mask portrayed,
Concealing scars, deeply dismayed.
Beneath the facade, a silent plea,
For understanding, to set them free.
But whispers cruel, they twist and twine,
In darkest corners, where shadows dine.
Self-harm's whispers, a dangerous lure,
A desperate plea for pain to endure.
Manipulation's tangled snare,
A cry for help, too much to bear.
Yet in the midst, a flicker remains,
A spark of hope, through tearful stains.
So let us reach, with gentle hand,
To lift the burden, to understand.

For in this dance of pain and light,
We find the strength to win the fight.

Ayhan Battal (11)
The Academy Of St Nicholas, Liverpool

Breaking Blocks

Here I am,
Spawning in a new world,
Looking for materials
To stop me from being killed.

Night-time air fills the sky,
And lots of mobs are charging at me,
So I run into the closest cave,
The only one I can really see.

Living in a cave,
Desperate for a snack,
I look around full of hope,
But for miles, I'm surrounded by black.

I run out of the cave
To find it's daytime.
But when I turn around,
There it is, a giant slime.

I have to run,
Maybe to a village.
And when I'm safe,
It's my turn to pillage.

I walk out unharmed,
Richer than before.
I just hope they don't revolt,
But I'm ready to fight some more.

I decide to build a house
Out of the materials I gathered.
But after a couple of days pass,
I notice my house is weathered.

My mum shouts, saying dinner's ready,
And saying to turn off the game.
But now I leave my Minecraft character,
Oh, what a shame.

Connor Moore (12)
The Academy Of St Nicholas, Liverpool

Untitled

She walks on the street in her golden gown,
The people in the village clear a path for her to stroll down.
She looks at their shoes, mutters some words and carries on her walk,
As the others get back into their herds.
She makes her way through the cobbled path
That twists and turns as others pass.
She gets to the market, all eyes on her
Their eyes start to shimmer as they turn.
She looks through the eyes of a broken heart
And people who own a golden heart.
She looks through the eyes of sadness and sorrow
And the criminals who like and tend to 'borrow'.
She snaps out of the trance, the crowds start to calm.
So does her heart due to the place that she went.
Her mind started to change on her way home
She set things the right way.
She said hi to the people, they just stood in shock
She skipped down the path as she fell.
But she felt a warm hand in hers
Her heart was so fast, so was theirs,
They laugh together, and hand it hand
Show the people her bad mood is banned.

Evelyn Wild (11)
The Academy Of St Nicholas, Liverpool

Teenage Mind

A girl so blonde she's beyond,
Too busy to respond,
A princess with a magic wand,
Her bond with music is strong,
But sometimes she can be a devil when her thoughts level,
She goes mental although she could have potential,
She lets negative thoughts interfere,
She goes on long walks to escape her mind for a while,
She has a happy smile whilst hiding in denial,
Her appearance is all that matters,
As long as I'm pretty?
Have a nice style,
She finds people irritating and vile
But will dial their number if they need someone,
All her love drained out flying like a dove,
Mental health taking over, she just wants to be brave!
But she's so deeply loved by many around,
She asks why life has so many tasks,
But thanks herself for being the happiest,
And getting over all the times she covered her sadness with a happy mask.

O Moore (14)
The Academy Of St Nicholas, Liverpool

I Am Born

I am born,
And why do I cry?
To sever the cord,
Of my life support,
And forced to leave,
A maternal womb,
That shall be my eternal tomb.

I am born,
And why do I cry?
Into this purgatory,
Where the casque of steel,
Shields our eyes,
From the heaven's sombre skies.

I am born,
And why do I cry?
Where blood has become our wine,
Lest we drink to forgotten lore,
When man could instead, forfeit the world
And nurture his ivory soul.

I am born,
And why do I cry?
When finally I can open my eyes,
And yet be the more blind,
Where blue shall colour the flags up high
We must drag through shackles and ties.

I am born,
And why do I cry?
Where hands of lust
Grope and buy,
Where hands of love
Shall surely die.

I am born,
And why do I cry?
When the sun is but a dying ember,
And Juliet dies with her,
With Romeo as her killer,
While her heart, within us all, shall wither.

Skye Ainsworth (14)
The Academy Of St Nicholas, Liverpool

Untitled

In shadows once a hero stood so tall,
A champion for justice, heeding the call.
But whispers of power twisted his mind
Into darkness, a path he'd soon find.
Once adorned in armour, gleaming and bright,
Now tainted, consumed by the endless night.
The hero's heart, once pure and strong,
Corrupted by ambition everything gone wrong.
A tragic metamorphosis unfolds,
As virtue crumbles, the villain's story moulds.
The corpse now tattered, symbol of decay,
A hero lost astray.
The city that once named his noble name,
Now trembles in fear at his ruthless flame.
With every step, the villain leaves a scar,
A fallen hero who strayed too far.
The battle within, a turbulent war,
Between the hero he was and the villain's core.
A tragic tale of a noble soul's descent,
Into darkness where virtue is spent.

Savannah-Rose Rawlings-Baig (11)
The Academy Of St Nicholas, Liverpool

Nora's Happy End

At the start, everything was great
Until it was not.
Day after day
Everything was grey.
First it was love
He should love but not for long,
He was manipulating me through the world views,
Through the people around us and through threads...

People were on his side.
My family and friends maybe even his...
"But he is acting nice," they said.
"But he is just different," they said...

Even my family was guilty.
They forced me into it and loved it while it lasted.

My friends were the same but some were not...

But justice, light and happiness,
Flourished when he broke it off,
"I am bored," he said
And for once I nodded and agreed
"Me too, from you."
And I was happy,
I cut them all off and now found happiness in new people...

Sonya Balkandzhievo (13)
The Academy Of St Nicholas, Liverpool

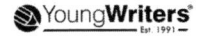

Foxy (FNAF)

In Freddy Fazbear's Pizza Place,
Friendliness fills the room,
Everyone here feels safe,
But soon will come a doom.

"Foxy is a monster,"
Is what they say,
They hide in a locker,
To stay away.

They built me with love,
And parts they can find,
Now they think I have a psychopathic mind.

They call us murderers,
But we were possessed,
So who's the determiner,
Come up and confess.

How they hate our ways,
Hate our praise,
They want to raise,
The amount of disgrace.

What have I done to deserve this?
Where is the love?
I just receive a swarm of fists,
Will there be a guide, a dove?

Bad day, good day or sad day,
Sunset or rain,
Happiness or pain,
None of them will remain,
Please let this end...

Mymoona Al-Zoubi (12)
The Academy Of St Nicholas, Liverpool

Untitled

The girl,
she wakes up
glueing her mask to her face
hoping that is all people will see,
but she knows...
she knows she can't keep doing this.
She knows that what is under the mask
is slowly killing her.
The solemn girl takes a look
at herself
in the mirror
every day, thinking
why me?
Every day, she goes to school,
her mask laughing and smiling
but behind it,
she hurts.
Every day, she gets home,
her mum and dad arguing,
thinking,
another stab behind my mask.
Every day, she listens to her friends' problems,
thinking,
give me a break.

At the end of every day,
she goes to her room,
sits at her desk,
looks in the mirror
and removes her mask,
thinking,
someone love me.

Ilana Herd (12)
The Academy Of St Nicholas, Liverpool

Broken

Finally, everyone is gone
Now I can go and yawn
It's been busy today
To my uncomfortable dismay.

I'm very tired
I'm about to retire
Crash, a window breaks
I jump and shake.

I hear them waiting
Hearing nothing but talking
Then my body shakes
Now I'm really awake.

They're breaking me
One, two, three
I scream in agony
But no one hears.

I'm not a lock
I feel like a mock
My body feels shattered
As away they pattered.

I feel transfixed
As I know I can't be fixed
I can't be awakened
As I know I'm broken.

Broken is what I am
Since I have no jam
All is lost for me
There's no future for what I see.

Broken is what I am
Broken is how I remain.

Naina Aggarwal (13)
The Academy Of St Nicholas, Liverpool

Conquering My Dream

As I took the biggest decision of my life to be a pilot,
I began running towards it
As my heart fell in love with the sky.
The sky as vast as the ocean.
Unpredictability made me an ambitious person.
Through the blooming of ambition I had grown drastically
Exams came and went
But not my ambition for the sky.
As my ambition grew bigger,
I passed the sea of exams, obstacles and failure
As I passed them,
I sat in a rough and majestic seat,
The controls felt hard but my heart was soft.
I set to the sky,
The feeling was timid but confident,
The sky as beautiful as the heavens
As I conquered my ambition
It felt congenial
The sound of engines dazzled at 37,000 feet
As I achieved the dream of a lifetime
I continued... but never gave up.

Sathyadharmaraj Shyam (14)
The Academy Of St Nicholas, Liverpool

What Once Was There

They say there is hope, a home will soon come
They say there is hope, the war will be won
But the bread is turning stale, the camp is now full
And the glint in our eyes is beginning to dull.

I was once back at home, all tucked up in bed
And visions of fairies dance through my head
My mother downstairs and my father is home
But now I am hungry and chilled to the bone.

I was once back at home, my toys in a row
With my old flowery dress and a matching bow
All these things I once took for granted
Now I am here with only a blanket.

They say there is hope, a home will soon come
They say there is hope, the war will be won
For the sky is not yet dark, and the war is not yet done
So why should I cry when my life has just begun?

Anya Lock (12) & Annette Riley (13)
The Academy Of St Nicholas, Liverpool

Alone

Alone.
A word used to describe a certain feeling of emptiness,
A feeling of isolation.
Most people perceive being alone as a negative trait,
Not me.
I've been alone for so long that I find comfort in it.
Being engulfed in the empty space is soothing,
It's cold and dark
And I don't have to put up a front with it.
You see, the empty space doesn't judge,
In fact, it doesn't say anything,
It just lets you live.
I guess most people would feel uncomfortable
With having nothing but yourself taking up space,
Paying attention to your own breath,
Finding fault in each inhale and exhale.
For me, it's the opposite,
Being alone doesn't help me find my faults
Because other people already do it for me.

Matt Johnson (13)
The Academy Of St Nicholas, Liverpool

The Savage Humans I've Designed

Endless debris is what I can see
From the savage humans I've designed
Beauty is crumbling, animals are scuttling
From the savage humans I've designed
Death's increase no longer peace
Plastic piling, they are almost dying
From the savage humans I've designed
How could I design such awful creatures
With such good features that are no longer preachers of me?
Foolish am I? For letting the world in their care
So they made it theirs with no hope to spare
The humans I led to do my work shall be enthroned and rich
But the humans that scorn that tore me shall be the ones to burn
Ungodly acts the creatures do to ruin my world once more
They better be ready, they better be moral
Before the world is at death's door.

Annice Damulina (13)
The Academy Of St Nicholas, Liverpool

The Haunted House

Depression is like a haunted house,
Except you're the only person in it,
Everybody else the ghosts,
Nothing feels real anymore,
The feeling of derealisation, you can see people,
But it's just like they can't see you,
The clouded fog inside your muffled brain,
It lingers, always there,
Why can't I just turn it off?
The demon has taken my brain,
Taken my feelings,
Keeping me up at night, panicked, worried,
Tears begin to roll out,
The taste of salty nothingness,
The storm rages on stronger than before,
My knees go weak,
All I want is for the world to swallow me up,
Then I fade into nothingness,
Disappearing into my troubled background,
My empty childhood,
When does this all end?

Amelia Brennan-Cullingford (12)
The Academy Of St Nicholas, Liverpool

The Future Is Mine

As I was wandering through life,
Seeking hope for a future,
I looked left and right,
Underneath the dark night sky,
Seeking refuge and a place to call my home.
I felt the trees, as dark as the night sky, wailing,
And the sea, angry, refusing to be still.
The air smelt like sulphur,
Burning through my lungs,
I refused to stop and give up amidst challenges,
To have a fulfilled and achieved life.
Finally, I was there.
A hope and a future right in front of my eyes.
This future I see,
Can't be without the help of my teachers and mentors,
On whose shoulders I stand,
Through thick and thin.
Yes, alas! The future is here and now,
With the 'I can' mentality.
The future is mine.

Ruby Barnabas (12)
The Academy Of St Nicholas, Liverpool

The Rise

As I walked out of my second class,
I was greeted by bad looks and stares,
Their stares got to me, even before they opened their mouths.
"Eee, look at this thing,"
"Okay, what did I do, oh my lord,"
"Exist,"
That one broke me.
As they kept going
I waited for their leave,
Then they did
And I broke down in tears that were enough to make an ocean.
I ran to the office,
I snitched,
But now I've put myself in more danger,
Messages fly through my phone,
"You're made, ugly you,"
"Built like a stick."
I told my mum and she assured me I'm okay,
I looked in her eyes and she was crying.
Her tears broke me more than the comments.

Tallulah Rasmussen (11)
The Academy Of St Nicholas, Liverpool

Education And Success

I am Albert Einstein, you may know me very well
But I've got a lot to tell
Have you wondered about the way life goes?
Well, I'm here to tell you how it's done
It's easy to plan the future if you have a passion
But you gotta be compassionate
The main key is confidence and knowledge
As you may learn to know
The way life works
Education is one top priority
Otherwise, you may be guilty
You'll have to fix your life like a picture that is tilted
As you may acknowledge everything to complete your passion
Say goodbye to procrastination
And hello to success and efficiency
Hope you now know the way it's done
Get your procrastination ready to be gone.

Serah Maria Anson (12)
The Academy Of St Nicholas, Liverpool

Teacher, Oh Teacher

Every day I go home stressed,
depressed about what's coming next.
Always make a good impression on the principal,
by bringing in moral principles.
I can't stop the situation
sick and tired of keeping my emotions,
wishing to be appreciated,
tired of being disrespected,
wanting to be respected.

They might not know,
but the joy of seeing my students thrive,
makes me feel alive,
Though they are very inquisitive,
They are also innovative.

I shudder at the helpful occupation,
I want to leave but I want the conversation,
The conversation of being respected, loved and accepted,
finally recognised for the knowledge I pass around.

Shalom Joseph (11)
The Academy Of St Nicholas, Liverpool

My Life Through My Eyes

Why, why? Every day, an argument comes, hooray!
Why, why do I hide my sadness over happiness?
Why, why does everyone hate me? With vex I hit and with
Sadness I crawl through life.
Why, why am I embarrassed with my personality?
Why, why does self-hatred drown me?
Why, why do... I lie?
Why, why, why do I not let myself control me and
Let others use me like a puppet?
I am not a thing!
I am not seen!
I am not a ghost!
See me. Listen to me!
I lose every day, like a ghost I drift through my life,
Dodging the bullets that come,
Drifting through lessons,
I run, away from the darkness that chases me every day.

Why?
Why?
Why...?

Marco Meloro (11)
The Academy Of St Nicholas, Liverpool

My Mum

My mum, an independent and brave person.
When she enjoys her glorious life,
She chose to give birth to me at twenty-two.
To top it off, she got divorced at twenty-three.

She took me to her house from my dad.
In recent years, she often told me,
"In the 7 years since my divorce,
I went through an emotional low."
I always think something like,
"If she didn't choose me, maybe her life would be better."

I once asked her this question.
Her answer made my eyes fill with tears.
"Your presence doesn't bother me.
On the contrary, it brings me a lot of happiness."
I just want to say,
I love you, my mum.

Ying Ki Yanki Chow (12)
The Academy Of St Nicholas, Liverpool

Behind The Smiles

Behind the smiles, I feel pain
Jealous, anxious and scared
Projecting my pain
I know, deep down, my pain causes pain
If only they knew I feel the same.

My friends aren't my real friends
I feel lost
If only I could be found
So I am not lost.

My insecurities are my confidence
But also my fear
I wish it could be true
Instead of making people live in fear.

I victimised people to show my strengths
Bullying and harassment are part of my defence
If only the victim knew I'd experienced this too
I've physically hurt people, and mentally too.

If only they knew, I've been there too.

Lily-Sue Shields (11)
The Academy Of St Nicholas, Liverpool

Our Home, The Jungle, Their Land, The Factories

Our home, the jungle,
Only disturbed by a knock or tumble.
Our home, the jungle,
Few visitors aren't a rumble.
Our home, the jungle,
Many plants, such as fungi.
Our home, the jungle,
Has recently gained a rumble?
Our home, the jungle,
Has recently seen new species stumble.
Our home, the jungle,
Is being taken away by a shovel.
Their land, the factories,
Smells of batteries.
Their land, the factories,
Taking our land is one of their victories.
Their land, the factories,
Seeing our land and friends can only be fantasies.
Their land, the factories,
We could never imagine such tragedies.

Louise Garvey (12)
The Academy Of St Nicholas, Liverpool

2024

It is 2024,
Women have rights
Sexuality is no longer frowned upon
People of a different race have freedom,
Political views are changing,
But yet they are still odd,
I've watched people snarl as someone prays,
I've watched stares as people of the same gender hold hands.

It is 2024
Can we make this normal?
Can we make freedom for who you love
With no stares or snarls?
Can we make believing in God cool?
Maybe that is someone's saviour,
Can we treat people equally?
That is all I ask,
No more snarls and more smiles,
No more prejudice and more pride.
It is 2024. Come on!

Isla Atkinson-Pye (13)
The Academy Of St Nicholas, Liverpool

My Miserable Life

Every day I walk, until I feel my legs being cut off.
Another hopeless day,
You're not breaking the system if the waiter who brings your food will never try that taste.

While I work, I think when this injustice will come to an end.
I run, trying to be free,
Trying to see.
I am a miserable rat trying to survive in the abyss,
At the end of the line,
But my boss is in their prime.

What I eat every day is rationed,
When will I leave this situation?
I am like a cow,
Working hard and not getting any reward, somehow.
I am poor, a hopeless case,
Will one day I finally have a chance?

Lorena Soares (13)
The Academy Of St Nicholas, Liverpool

The Lonely Window

I was sitting on my ledge,
Whilst life was passing me by,
I saw a weird-shaped hedge,
Then I started to cry.

I thought, what an ugly life,
To be trapped behind a frame,
This is what life is like,
It will always be the same.

I thought about the times,
When I saw them pass,
I wish that I could celebrate,
But I'm made of glass.

I thought about the times,
They were filled with joy,
I wanted to join,
But I'm not a boy.

I'm just a window,
That people see through,
I'm not a flamingo,
But people never see what they're meant to.

Delilah Williams (12)
The Academy Of St Nicholas, Liverpool

Let's End Racism

Let's end racism.
Because it makes someone feel like they're in a prism.
It makes someone feel bad and sad.
And it is also ruining their lives.
Let's end racism.
Don't judge a book by its cover.
We all know it.
So why do we do it over and over?
Racism is not cool.
So, let's treat everyone as a jewel.
No room for judgement, no room for fear.
Let compassion and understanding be near.
With open minds and hearts, so true.
We'll build a world where racism is through.
Let's end racism.
It's time to unite and come together.
And let our light shine.

Moise Bwaka (12)
The Academy Of St Nicholas, Liverpool

The Life Of A Man

In youth's embrace, a tender start,
A man unfolds a work of art,
Childhood dreams, like seeds sown,
In the life vast garden, they've grown.

Adventure shaped by lessons learned,
Through every twist, a page turned,
From playful laughter to earnest skies.

The teenage years, were a wild ride,
In passion, fears and joy, he'd confide,
With every stumble, each hope leap,
A journey of discovery, secrets to keep.

As seasons change, and time does too,
He matures, gains strength anew,
Reflection of the boy he'd been,
Now painted with wisdom seen.

Aiham Halloudi (12)
The Academy Of St Nicholas, Liverpool

A Prisoner Of My Own Insanity (I Think)

Tick-tock, tick-tock.
That stupid clock doesn't stop.
I'm strapped up in this arm thing.
I can't even remember my own name.
Never mind what this is called.
All I know is it ties my arms back from touching anything.

What is my name again?
Hmm... shut up Bradly.
It's not Mr Poopy Pants!
Bradly sits in the corner of my room.
Laughing at me.

Tick-tock, tick-tock.
Not that stupid game again!
Bradly's telling me to take my tablets again.
Tablets? What even is that?
Tablets. Haha. That's a funny word.
What was I saying again?

Jessica Alvers (13)
The Academy Of St Nicholas, Liverpool

Through The Eyes Of A Pup / Dear Margaret

My tail wiggled happily aside
Waiting for my owner to arrive,
Suddenly I heard a loud pop
I thought it was our neighbour dropping a rock.

Running towards the sound is something I regret,
And there, lying, was dear Margaret.
Thought she was sleeping, so I ran outside
Running around but something felt wrong.

I jumped over the fence to get help for Mum.
I saw a person on the other side of the road.
Guess who ran there, limping like a frog.
Middle of the street.
Everything went black.
The last thing I saw was a light,
And my last tear dropping felt sad.

Aniela Dominte (12)
The Academy Of St Nicholas, Liverpool

Nature's Symphony

In a world of vibrant green, where nature's beauty gleams,
There stood a girl with black hair and eyes like rich brown streams.
She walked among the trees with a heart so full of grace,
Embracing the Earth's wonders in every place.
Her footsteps left no trace as she wandered the land,
A gentle touch upon the earth with love and care at hand.
She listened to the whispers of the wind among the leaves,
And danced with flowing rivers as they shimmered and weaved.
For in the eyes of this girl, with black hair and brown eyes,
With hope for a greener world where harmony never dies.

Yan Situ (11)
The Academy Of St Nicholas, Liverpool

Through My Mother's Eyes

When I see my mother's eyes,
I see love, like a dove and the warmth of a hug.
I see compassion, like an angel always helping people.
I see caring, like a nurse attentively taking care of the patient.

My mum, a responsible, smart person.
When she just got married,
She gave birth at twenty-nine.
Her tireless life was about to begin.

My mum, an attentive person.
When her daughter gets sick,
She thinks, *is she taking the mick?*

I've looked into my mother's eyes,
The love I've seen within my eyes,
I will see for evermore.

Man Chun June Tsoi (12)
The Academy Of St Nicholas, Liverpool

Amongst The World

I am here, I am far, I am everywhere,
I swim through the trees,
I simply help out the bees,
I can be strong, yet I can be weak,
I am happy when the sky goes blue,
Yet I love the mixed hue of the pinks and reds,
But life can be bleak, even at
The highest peak.
I am sick, I am ill, the world is upset,
I am stuck this way,
No matter what day,
I am beyond help, becoming darker each day,
My flow of life is getting slower,
The bees now hate me, each flower becoming duller,
I have no more power, nor breeze,
Yet I am still amongst the world.

Alyssa Mercer (14)
The Academy Of St Nicholas, Liverpool

They Only Love Me When I Change

Why me?
I'm hated,
For nothing,
Why don't you love me?
Why don't you love me the way I am?
Please tell me what I've done wrong,
I'm lonely,
I thought you would help,
But instead, you did the opposite!
Please tell me what's wrong!
Why do you hate me?
You make me feel lonely!
Tell me why!
I've done everything you asked for!
I'm broken!
You told me to change, but I have!
Everything!
What have I done wrong that made you hate me?
Love me now!
Why did you do this?
Why me?

Raseal Alser (11)
The Academy Of St Nicholas, Liverpool

Behind The Scenes

Every day it is the same
People chase me and call my name
Sometimes I feel like I just want to run away
To a place where I can peacefully stay
All anyone wants from me is my money
Or just to call me their honey
I prefer my old past
But it has just gone too fast
I miss my private space
But sometimes you change your place.

In life, when it's done it's done
I can't even see my mum
Without being harassed
Or asked about my class
This is all getting on my nerves
I don't know how but I can lure.

Nojus Akelaitis (11)
The Academy Of St Nicholas, Liverpool

The Thief

The thief, sweeping through the alleys,
From side to side,
Not scared to run into a gang,
He's fly and also sly,
He looks up and sees police helicopters in the sky,
He's scared for his life, worrying about his wife,
And through his brain, thinking
What have I done?
All he can do is run,
He's never giving up,
Next second, he sees the police, and he's like,
Yup!
But he's not finished,
He's not giving up,
But through the gaps, he sees police saying,
Bonjour.

Kacper Dobranski (12)
The Academy Of St Nicholas, Liverpool

Love Or Hate

This Earth I live on, I do sport
And if I'm supposed to eat tomato pasta and throw it away
I'm always getting caught.

At school, I'm needing education
To follow my inspiration
On social media, everyone's talking about Marmite
I take a bite and it doesn't taste right.

The monarchy means it forms a government
And the monarch at the lead
And I don't really understand indeed.

Social media is full of influencers
Who copy each other
But they never care for my mother.

Louis Fell (12)
The Academy Of St Nicholas, Liverpool

The Decaying Computer

From the on-and-offs every day,
From the enter key presses every six minutes,
From the CPU overloading every day,
From the GPU overheating every day,
I decay day by day.

From the incorrect passwords,
From the raging user,
From the hard drive corruptions,
From the space bar, W, A, S and D getting smacked,
I decay day by day.

From the game downloads,
From the speakers blasting,
From the USB ports getting weaker and weaker,
From the awful Ethernet connections,
I decay day by day.

Liam Johnson (12)
The Academy Of St Nicholas, Liverpool

Nature's Beauty

The Earth, our home, so vast and wide,
With nature's wonders side by side.
Mountains tall and holes deep,
A world where secrets are meant to keep.

Flowers blooming, colours so bright,
Filling the air with sweet delight.

Nurturing life, far and near,
Forests green, a peaceful retreat,
Where animals roam, their home complete.

Let's cherish this gift with all our might,
Protecting nature day and night.
For in the beauty of the environment we see,
A reflection of our unity.

Thrina Datta (14)
The Academy Of St Nicholas, Liverpool

Destruction Comes To Last

I'm a big ball of flames, not a fan of fame,
I'm surrounded with planets only full of plants,
As I look closer, I notice the plants dying and people crying.

There are words and desires,
There's destruction and hate,
The Earth is dying and no one is helping!

The people must stop making the fire and smoke,
Others must be kind,
The hate and tragedies caused murder!

There's not much they can change,
But they can at least acknowledge the planet they're making!

Samanta Garklava (13)
The Academy Of St Nicholas, Liverpool

War

I can see the soldiers
Waving bye to their
Worried-faced parents
As I make my way
To what used to be my home.

In the middle of the war
I heard a lot of bombs
And I could smell the fire
Which made me cough.

I could taste my tears
And the bitter air
I saw more people shouting
To shoot more bombs
Which made me fear.

In the end, people were taken away
Some were left on the ground
Dead for their family to get them
At least I'm safe.

James Ahmed (12)
The Academy Of St Nicholas, Liverpool

Am I Really?

Am I really free if I can't control my humbleness?
Locked behind bars of my own happiness
I am the greed and the hole for their needs
Plagued by thoughts of destruction
Manipulated the resurrection of angels of the stars
The claws embrace my weathered body
Strangling the darkness, pouring like a dying teapot
Staggered breaths
Shaky skin
I shone the light into their eyes
Blinded by my horrible light
But they need it like a poppy of the war
Am I really as bad as I say I am?

Jolie Guano (13)
The Academy Of St Nicholas, Liverpool

Fake Smile

Their faces shining bright like the sun.
But behind stands a dark shadow,
Their eyes flooding with tears.
Faking their happiness as everyone seems just fine,
But behind their smiling face is the bully.
Their mental health disappears,
While their fear is shown,
So they hide their face with their phone,
That never helps as comments start to rise.
And they don't know because of the fake smile,
You never know what someone is going through.
And maybe next time it will be you.

Poppy Wild (11)
The Academy Of St Nicholas, Liverpool

Where Now?

As I watch my own funeral, I think to myself,
Or did I say it and nothing came out?
Where now?

As I see all the people I know mourning,
All I think is,
Where now?

As I think how trapped I am, all I say is,
Where now?

As I taste the freedom on the
Tip of my tongue, I think,
Where now?

As the thought sets in, all I say is,
Where now?

As I see the light, I say,
Where now?

Evie Killen (12)
The Academy Of St Nicholas, Liverpool

Untitled

In shadows cast, secrets unfold
A web of deceit, stories untold
Betrayals dance, a twisted affair
Hearts burn apart, beyond repair.

Whispers of cries, echoes of mistrust
A fragile bond shattered, turning to dust
Promises broken, trust skips away
Leaving behind heartache that will forever stay.

In the aftermath, wounds start to heal
But scars remain, a reminder so real
Forgiveness sought, a difficult choice
To mend what's broken, to find inner voice.

Paulie Conroy
The Academy Of St Nicholas, Liverpool

Life Of A Teen

A teen, a teen
Who always suffers in silence
A teen
Who keeps the blistering part hidden
A teen
Which their parents think don't have feeling
A teen
Who keeps an ecstatic face,
Everywhere they go
The brave teen who worries a lot
Who is subconscious
Always feeling excluded, frustrated, depressed
Stressed, bored and scared to move forward
'Cause they don't know what's coming next
I am now asking a question
What should we teens do?

Oluwaferanmi Kolawole (11)
The Academy Of St Nicholas, Liverpool

The War That Shouldn't Have Happened

It's sometime in March '23
My squadron is fleeing for safety
We have been deployed to the
Ukrainian coast as our
Comrades in the fire roast.

Bullets and bombs come
From the sky
And as wildlife goes extinct
It'd take less than a blink
To watch everything crumble.

With the greenery gone
And the fire departed
A lonesome poppy grows
In the marshland in the middle
Where life used to thrive
And known as where it started.

Evan Kelly (13)
The Academy Of St Nicholas, Liverpool

Sunak's Shadow

In Britain's street, I shake my head,
Sunak's choices, they leave me dead.
His decisions, both dark and bright,
I worry I might not sleep tonight.

Yet, in the mix of a hopeful gleam,
Measures taken like a sunbeam.
Amidst the struggles, there's a glint of light,
Sunak's positivity shining bright tonight,
Yet still, the negativity casts its shadow despite.

The shadow grows longer, day by day,
Job losses rise, and uncertainty thrives...

Saja Harrud (12)
The Academy Of St Nicholas, Liverpool

Police Are Heroes

Police are emergency services, that help people from criminals,
Police are saving adults and children from danger,
I am reading a poem about the police,
Now I need to get back to work,
I need to use my bravery in a good way,
So I can help move people from danger,
I was walking on a street,
I saw how a young person wanted to get money from an old man,
I started to run there and helped the old man,
He said, "Thanks."
I was happy helping people as a hero.

Refat Muyedinov (13)
The Academy Of St Nicholas, Liverpool

Just The Child

I hear the shouting,
The banging on the walls.
I really want to help,
But I can't do any more.
After all,
I'm only the child.

The tiny disagreements,
The big, massive brawls.
I think I can fix everything,
My parents would disagree.
After all,
I'm just the child.

The flaming hot glares,
Exchanged across the table.
It puts me in the middle,
But I can't help.
After all,
I'm just the child.

Talia Elmahdi (13)
The Academy Of St Nicholas, Liverpool

The Life Of Jerry...

I wake up in the morning,
sun blaring
birds cheeping
I have to wait for someone,
it's a new morning,
I wait and wait... nothing,
time is so slow it feels like decades,
I'm pacing back and forward,
suddenly, there she is,
all I can do is bark back,
louder and louder, I am so excited,
I get loves then off she goes,
every day she left, I couldn't help but wait,
every noise bark but no human,
when will she be back...?

Lillie-May Wong-Morgan (12)
The Academy Of St Nicholas, Liverpool

Through The Eyes Of Messi

Messi on the ball, he dribbles past one defender
There are now three
OMG, he's on a roll
That's four and five
OMG, he's one-to-one with the keeper
If he scores, he wins the Champions League final
He takes a breath
The keeper is getting ready for the shot
Messi lines it up
He shoots, he scores
The crowd goes wild
Messi wins Barcelona
The Champions League
He is truly the greatest of all time
The GOAT, Lionel Messi.

Harley Magee (11)
The Academy Of St Nicholas, Liverpool

Real Eyes

Around the globe, where people reside,
But only so many happy lives,
A prisoner, a hostage, a murderer too,
But real eyes, realise,
That I'm unhappy too.

Throughout the streets,
And down the road,
There is a family you might know,
With laughter, cheers and so much fun,
Now real eyes, realise,
Something must be done.

It could cost an arm or a leg,
Or maybe both,
But now, it is time for development and growth.

Michael Kanoniuk (13)
The Academy Of St Nicholas, Liverpool

The Refugee

One stormy night,
It really wasn't a delight,
It was the shock of my life,
It came with a fright,
Bombs in every direction,
No safety in any section,
Gunshots fired,
I was very tired,
Hiding in terror,
Body shivering like the cold,
My family was nowhere to be seen,
This was somewhere you have never been,
My door got booted down,
The next minute I was found,
They dragged me away,
I closed my eyes and prayed...

Frankee Perry (11)
The Academy Of St Nicholas, Liverpool

We're Not Different Because We're All Human

We are all human,
No matter what gender,
We're all the same,
It doesn't matter at all.
We can be friends with someone of a different race,
As long as they are kind.
We can love someone no matter their religion.
So why do we judge people just because they are different?
Maybe it's because we 'try to fit in'
But we shouldn't care about people's opinions
Because at the end of the day,
We are all the same.

Aseel Alser (11)
The Academy Of St Nicholas, Liverpool

The Hypocritical War

I saw her smiling brightly with her big dark eyes,
Flashing her teeth to show how happy she was,
I noticed something wrong,
I felt the uneasiness of that smile,
The uneasiness only someone suffering the same felt,
I felt it,
The agonising war of fighting with yourself in another realm,
'The Realm of the Mental'
They told us we were special but I knew deep down,
We were burning from the pressure of our image and to belong.

Toluwanimi Kolawole (14)
The Academy Of St Nicholas, Liverpool

I Am A Mother

I was naive
I was selfish
All I cared about was me
I never thought of the special one
Until the day I felt you within me.

It was strange but sweet
Annoying but warm
I couldn't accept it
But neither ignore it.

I started worrying about you
Caring about you
And loving you unconditionally.

Although you were small
But still changed my whole life
Even though it was hard
But you made it worth it.

Usra Siddiqui (13)
The Academy Of St Nicholas, Liverpool

Beneath The Veil Of The Way

In fields where silence now does reign,
Where once the din of war's refrain,
Lay shadows of a sombre past,
Echoes of the bugle's blast.

A land once lush, now scarred and bare,
Tells tales of sorrow, loss, despair.
Where flowers bloom, so too did fall,
The bravest soul, who gave their all.

Amidst the chaos, fear and strife life.
For freedom's light, for justice call,
They stood united,
Brave and tall.

Yasrib Siddiqui (12)
The Academy Of St Nicholas, Liverpool

Toxic Relationship

One fight here, one fight there,
One fight everywhere,
We seem to do it all the time,
And no one recognises it's a crime,
But when I go outside with the bruises,
I can never seem to hide,
I don't see the point of being alive,
Every day when he looks at me,
It makes me want to look away,
I would want to start with a fresh life,
But he wants to pull me away,
What can I do?
What can I say just to keep the man away?

Briana Silva (12)
The Academy Of St Nicholas, Liverpool

From A To The GOAT

I am just a goat, I'm not the greatest of all time.
I am just a goat, that's what everyone says, but I believe in myself.
I am not a goat, I am *the* goat.
And I feel that I am the greatest of all time.
I taste the resilience in myself and I am going to have trophies on my shelf.
I can see some people saying, "You are the GOAT."
I can hear from inside myself.
I am the Greatest Of All Time!

Giancarlo Pili (12)
The Academy Of St Nicholas, Liverpool

A Scouser's Footballing Dream

This dream was impossible
But it became possible
By getting scouted by Everton
To getting signed for Liverpool.

People said I couldn't do it
But I proved them wrong
From a shy boy from Anfield
To a confident boy playing for Liverpool.

I shone on the world's biggest stages
And became one of the best Scousers to play for Liverpool
So that is how the Scouser's footballing dream became true.

Leighton Yates (12)
The Academy Of St Nicholas, Liverpool

The Game Of Cat And Mouse

My eyes are everywhere,
Slowly dragging her in.
She will never be alone,
Let the games begin.

It doesn't matter where I go,
I feel his burning gaze on me.
As I pace back and forth, to and fro,
The voice in my head screams, "Who even is he?!"

Here I am once again,
Standing in front of her house.
Her hazel eyes lock onto mine,
There's my little mouse.

Madeleine Wileman-Duckworth (13)
The Academy Of St Nicholas, Liverpool

I'm Just A Nurse

I'm just a nurse,
You ring me when you need,
I'll pick you up off your feet.

Whenever I'm around,
I'll help you calm down.
Not only here for your family
Or friend, I'm here for you because
You're suffering as much as them.

If a person passes,
They say, "It's not your fault."
But I've done everything in my power
So is it really all I could have done?

Hannah Majewska (13)
The Academy Of St Nicholas, Liverpool

Cyberbullied

C arefully I walk to the dreaded school
Y oung cheers fill the streets
B ang, the notifications ring on my phone
E choing in my ears
R inging, ringing the hate goes
B ang, it goes again
U rges to run away
L ouder and louder
"L eave me alone!" I would cry
I wish for it to stop
E choing repeatedly
D own the corridors I go.

Seren Egan (12)
The Academy Of St Nicholas, Liverpool

Behind The Mask

Another day walking to school,
Sweat on my collar.
Another day feeling sick to my stomach.
What are they going to do?

Another day being kicked to the ground
As they laugh with pure joy.
Another day with bloodshot eyes,
But I can't cry because I'm not man enough.

Another day feeling like they're never going to stop.
Another day makes me feel worthless.
Another day with no ending.

Mollie Haresnape (14)
The Academy Of St Nicholas, Liverpool

Kim Kardashian's Mind

Being an influencer feels amazing,
Having people look up to you is one of the best feelings ever,
There are many people out there who I have to make proud,
I can't let them down,
Can't let them down,
The weight of the world is on my shoulders,
Yet I must cover it,
I can't keep the mask on my face any longer,
Can't hide how I feel,
But people are counting on me,
I must please them.

Darcie Corser (13)
The Academy Of St Nicholas, Liverpool

The Expedition Of Life

Ah, being a teenager, a time of growth and change,
navigating life's twists and turns, feeling a little strange.
Exploring new horizons, discovering who you are,
with dreams in your heart, reaching for the stars.

Your emotions run wild like a roller-coaster ride,
from laughing to tears, it's quite the wild tide.
Friendships forged, memories made,
in the flurry of youth, an adventure to be played.

Jan Abdu (11)
The Academy Of St Nicholas, Liverpool

The Magic Eyeball

My eye sees the world through love and grace
From bustling streets to nature's embrace
My eye sees the world through anger and hate
Through schools where students must come late.

My eye sees the world as flat
But am I blind, or am I sat?
The world is so confusing
But I do find it quite amusing.

My eye sees the world through thick and thin
But I just need to give it in.

Csenge Kishonti (13)
The Academy Of St Nicholas, Liverpool

Love's Symphony

Love is like a shining star in the dark,
A gentle whisper,
A soft comforting embrace,
It's laughter, tears and moments pure and bright,
A bond that time nor distance can erase.

It's the holding hands and walking side by side,
A warm sensation that feels like home,
In love, our fears and doubts we shall gently conceal,
For in each other's arms,
We are safe and sound.

Ishita Chowdhury (12)
The Academy Of St Nicholas, Liverpool

Duffin

He stormed in the classroom,
As angry as could be,
The only thing he could see was messy floors,
And children in the corridors,
He sat down, looked up and gave a frown,
In comes the class clown,
The moment he goes to talk, the fire alarm goes off,
"Everybody calmly walk down the stairs."
All he could hear was the beeping from the radio,
By now his patience was very low.

Jessica Kaufman (13)
The Academy Of St Nicholas, Liverpool

I May Not Be Malala

I may not be Malala
But I'm sure she is super brave
I know she will thank Allah
I am thankful she was saved.

I may not have felt the pain
Those girls will be thankful
Her parents would have tears like the rain
I'm sure she is grateful.

I know she will inspire in years to come
But I may not be Malala
She loves to inspire for fun
She will be Malala.

Sam William Liddell (13)
The Academy Of St Nicholas, Liverpool

The Spy In Disguise

In the shadows, I sneak,
Picking targets, playing tricks,
Planning on who would be next,
From high above, in skies so blue,
With my aim so true,
With a concentrated gaze and no time to waste,
I took my shot,
Successfully, poo descends on the chosen one,
The battle's been won and the victim is stunned,
In the end, I'm just a bird,
And my victory will not be blurred.

Maegan Never (12)
The Academy Of St Nicholas, Liverpool

What Can We Do?

Running as fast as I can,
Screaming, crying and shouting.
Shaken voices come in a sudden,
Every minute, footsteps getting closer and closer.
People run through me, looking and searching.
I'm terrified with no choice but to stay silent.
Unrested nights,
Hungry days wishing for rescue.
Dared to escape with only one hope, my child.
But came hopeless, without a limb.

Charlotte Hon (13)
The Academy Of St Nicholas, Liverpool

Growing Up

When I was little, I would go outside
And make daisy chains in the grass.
When I was little, I would dress up
As different Disney characters.
Suddenly, everything changed.
I started to go on my phone a lot more.
I felt pressure to do well in school.
I felt like I had to do different things to fit in.
As a teen, almost every day is hard
But I can fight through this.

Phoebe Child (11)
The Academy Of St Nicholas, Liverpool

I Am Anne

I am Anne,
Not spoken to
But spoken about,
Crying and scared
I hear the shouts.

I am Anne,
Writing a book
Nowhere to move, we're stuck,
Going to bed, my mother's crying
Waking up, my religion is dying.

I am Anne,
A family, no friends
I hope my time never ends,
Lying here, having no fun
Goodbye, now my time is done.

Finlee Perry (13)
The Academy Of St Nicholas, Liverpool

Snow Days

I only come when it's cold
But to children, I am bold
I am snow
But I just want you to know
Don't cry when I go by
Just remember that I am fun
And that is no pun.

You can make snowballs with me
But if not, just let me be
Snow days come when it is cold
If your parents say no, then just be told
But if they say yes, I'll have you sold.

Sam Hughes (12)
The Academy Of St Nicholas, Liverpool

Love Or Hate

L ingering whispers of affection, pure.
O vercoming shadows, love is sure.
V exed by anger, hate my lure.
E choes of warmth, love's the cure.

Or...

H arsh words that string and separate,
A nguish follows in its wake.
T ender hearts can navigate,
E nding hate with love's embrace.

Luna Pacheco (13)
The Academy Of St Nicholas, Liverpool

Through Their Eyes

Through their eyes, I am strong
Through my eyes, I'm about to shatter
Through their eyes, I am beautiful
Through my eyes, I can't bear to look
Through their eyes, I can do it
Through my eyes, I can't even try
Peer pressure, stereotypes
It takes courage to see yourself how you really are
I wish I could see myself through their eyes.

Maria Ragone Lopes (11)
The Academy Of St Nicholas, Liverpool

Untitled

"Cold," they said... "Cold!" they said!
But truly, all I feel is... fear.
Fear at the sight of death.
Fear at the sight of being alone.
Yet the feeling 'cold' hasn't washed over me.
Is it a shock? No... It's much more.
Something I'm unable to overcome...
Survivor's guilt. Maybe it was never meant to be...

Omran Alhussein (11)
The Academy Of St Nicholas, Liverpool

Trapped

I bang on the wall, but it just won't fall.
I scream and I scratch and I claw.
My head ached as I walked to the door
And knocked just once more.
The pain in my stomach, and the pain in my heart,
I tried but it would not fall apart.
I cried and looked at my sore hands, bereft,
But there was no hope here, there was no hope left.

Darcy Bate (12)
The Academy Of St Nicholas, Liverpool

It's Not True

There's so much
I watch from the eyes
Of a small fish.

I could suffer the worst
But everyone's bigger
So they matter more
I watch from the eyes
Of a forgotten soul.

They all say
It matters
But we all know
It does not.

It's okay
I'm just a small fish anyway.

Matilda Kalita (11)
The Academy Of St Nicholas, Liverpool

Shadow In My Heart

Memories dance in the night
A bittersweet light
The grief silent as the night.

The tears slowly flow
As I lurk in the shadows
My heart loves the ember that resists
Through a mist
Of sorrow
I feel hollow.

A tribute for echoes around my head
Is cherished in my heart, yet I feel apart.

Nevin Kulangara Sabu (12)
The Academy Of St Nicholas, Liverpool

Fame

Fame is not happiness it's just loads of people with empty heads, but not me.
I'm just imprisoned in my own brain, with no way of escape.
Only fame you might wonder, but I have fame, money, fans?
Yes, but is it worth it?
The question goes around my brain every second.
Fame is not happiness, it's emptiness.

Berat Coskuncay
The Academy Of St Nicholas, Liverpool

The Beautiful Maple Tree

A freezing autumn
My hands cold with the wind
The sun covered by the clouds
I see you and your dreamy eyes
Brightening my path like an angel
The plants around you seem to bloom
And my heart singing like a beautiful bird
I knew my world had changed
Changed like never before
I just know I love you.

Giovanna Mileo (13)
The Academy Of St Nicholas, Liverpool

My Ocean

My ocean is deep,
My ocean is wide.
My ocean isn't being looked after,
And neither am I!

The rubbish is small,
But the rubbish is big,
Especially when my ocean is covered in it.

I can no longer swim,
Without a worry.
Because now I have to look out,
For the pollution ahead.

Jessica Bennett (13)
The Academy Of St Nicholas, Liverpool

Death In The Depths

I got arrested and sentenced to death
For killing three hostages when I was a hostage
It's my final day wondering, pondering
Wondering what I'm eating
My stomach churning like a wrench
Going near death
Waiting until the depths
Looking at the light
Waiting for the rise of my unforgiving night.

Arjin Ali (13)
The Academy Of St Nicholas, Liverpool

Ocean

Plastic, plastic, plastic,
My temperature change is drastic.
As the ice melts, I rise.
Minute by minute, hour by hour.

I rise, I rise, I rise.
The government made you change your way.
Will they do the damage?

One day, I will burst my banks
And I will be now off the end of the world.

Corey
The Academy Of St Nicholas, Liverpool

Anne Frank's Misery

Hostile and hidden,
Desperate for any signs of freedom,
Feeling anxious and terrified,
Counting the days and nights,
In a hidden room with bare lights,
Nervous about what's to happen,
The tension filling the room not flattening,
Waiting for the trauma to stop,
Hoping for the misery to end.

Aisha Abdillahi (12)
The Academy Of St Nicholas, Liverpool

Life Is Like A Book

Life is like a book
Each day is a new chapter
Each emotion is a new page
Each of my thoughts can be read
Like the pages of a life-filled book
Sometimes the pages are filled with joy
Other times sadness finds its way through
But through it all we find our way
Writing our own tale day by day.

Hollie Winterson (13)
The Academy Of St Nicholas, Liverpool

Flower

I am a flower,
I grow, I embrace but sometimes
I put down my face.
I'm happy, I'm bright, but sometimes
I have to pull through and fight.
Water me! Water me!
I need my water!
If you don't, it's completely out of order.
I blossom, I grow
I do human things like a pro!

Jazmin Atkinson (12)
The Academy Of St Nicholas, Liverpool

Through Their Eyes

Text after text,
People bullying through me,
Ashamed as ever,
Hopefully, no one looks at me,
The bullying not stopping,
The victim bawling,
When is it gonna stop?
Getting worse by the minute,
Why isn't the victim telling on the bully?
Imagine how the victim is feeling.

Joseph Myles (11)
The Academy Of St Nicholas, Liverpool

War Must Go

Innocent young people dying,
Trying to escape.
Mistaking their homes for trenches,
Clenching their belongings,
Drowning their attention to the noises,
The war must go.
All the bangs and explosions.
All the killing and dying.
We need to make peace.
The war must go.

Heidi Fane (12)
The Academy Of St Nicholas, Liverpool

Through Their Eyes

Steel bars confine dreams, aspirations lost.
silent footsteps on a path of concrete
surrounded by bars,
there's no way out,
I wish to escape,
desperate for freedom,
I want to go home,
but I won't be there anytime soon,
I'm anxious for what's to come.

Angel Moyo (12)
The Academy Of St Nicholas, Liverpool

Untitled

When the sun goes down,
It's my time to shine,
I am the biggest and brightest
In our night sky.

I glisten through your window
As I float up high.
I watch you dream
As I beam down on your streets.

I hide away from the sun,
As it ruins all my fun.

Heidi Harrison (12)
The Academy Of St Nicholas, Liverpool

Untitled

A pen and a book changed a kid's life,
May your hopes not reflect your fears,
Yesterday was bad, today is bad, that doesn't mean tomorrow is bad,
As a professional boxer and a YouTuber,
I was still afraid to be in the ring,
Until I heard the crowd shout my name.

Kasra Gohari (13)
The Academy Of St Nicholas, Liverpool

Orca

When I swim, everybody fears
Sometimes I hunt with smartness
When I swim, I watch out for nets
In case they take me from my home
My family is gone, my friends are no more
I'm left on my own with nobody to call
I wish they were here to hear their laugh

Adam Formby (12)
The Academy Of St Nicholas, Liverpool

Untitled

Face full of make-up,
Body like a dream
This is every little girl's dream.
Everyone thinks she looks like this,
Uh oh, Photoshop it is.
With a lot of plastic surgery, this is what it is,
Yet all of us want to look like this.

Amelia Gaines (11)
The Academy Of St Nicholas, Liverpool

Red Poppies

I stand in Ukraine's fields where poppies bloom.
I'm covered in blood and wounds.
I stand in sadness and gloom.
My friends have left me behind, so now it's here I lie.
Hoping someone will save me before I die.

Scott Pye (13)
The Academy Of St Nicholas, Liverpool

A Dog And His Owner

It's me and him forever,
His smile as bright as the sun,
He cannot see,
But that's why he has me.
I am his guide dog,
I love him more than anything,
In the world.
I am his guide dog.

Amelia Wells Roberts (12)
The Academy Of St Nicholas, Liverpool

The War Went On

The more the war went on,
The more that we were gone,
When we were packing,
More bombs were tapping,
As we were running,
We saw more people crying,
As we got away,
We sat then cried all day.

Bobby Blyth (11)
The Academy Of St Nicholas, Liverpool

Environment

In nature's embrace,
Let's take a stand,
Hand in hand,
Let's protect our land,
With every choice,
Let's be wise and kind,
For a greener future,
We'll surely find.

Demi Parker (12)
The Academy Of St Nicholas, Liverpool

My Crazy Day

In a world full of wagging tails and boundless glee,
There's a small, crazy pup
Named Ruby, you see.
With ear-like sails, she darts and dashes,
Leaving a trail of mischief in her crazy dashes.

Josh Feeley (13)
The Academy Of St Nicholas, Liverpool

Embracing Yourself

I am me
I grow from time to time
I embrace slowly
I have a heart full of love
That can fill you up with warmth
I can inspire
Because that is what I desire
I am kind and friendly.

Alaa Emziane (12)
The Academy Of St Nicholas, Liverpool

I Am A Football

I am a football
That gets kicked around
I'm used to score
But I am still hurt
Sometimes I even pop
Maybe I get kicked around
The smooth grass or sludgy grass.

Mustafa Mahmood (12)
The Academy Of St Nicholas, Liverpool

Life In A War

As I eat the last of my rations,
I shiver in the cold unforgiving night,
My house is in ruins,
And so is my life,
My family is dead,
I'm the only one alive.

Max Mercer (12)
The Academy Of St Nicholas, Liverpool

Bullying Of Darkness

In shadows cast, I shrink away,
From words that cut, from games they play.
Their laughter echoes, haunting still,
As loneliness becomes my will.

Daniel Kidd (13)
The Academy Of St Nicholas, Liverpool

Through My Eyes

Through the eyes of a baby their life is so bright,
Newly born, little hands, little small feet,
And a little face playing every day until those days were over.

Through the eyes of a toddler, they've just started nursery.
New surroundings and new people.
They've started learning and they've grown.
The world is still bright like summer days and everything feels free.

Through the eyes of a child they've started school.
Everything's bigger but they haven't noticed they've changed.
The world keeps spinning and things become different.

Through the eyes of a teenager, they've started high school and it's a new beginning.
Exams, tests, mocks, homework, revision and everything in-between.
But then they start to notice the smaller things.
Their body is changing and their peers are older.
When did this happen? When did this start?
My friends got prettier, but life got harder.
I wish I noticed the smaller things in life, I wish I was young again.

Marisa Becker (13)
The Hammond School, Chester

See The World

Some see it round, some see it flat,
You only see a little bit, created by God or not,
I see the world, through my specific lens,
Yours may be different, it really depends.

Through my eyes, the world is a cycle of deceit,
Taunting, teasing, tearing you down until you accept defeat,
Through older, wiser eyes, the world has fully changed,
For worse, or for better, it will never be the same.

Hidden faces behind phones, never fully seeing the world,
You should show yourself on social media and insults are hurled,
Teens hide behind a filter, wearing it like a mask,
Hiding their insecurities, and finally love them back.

But they fall in love with this stereotype of beauty,
Never knowing their beauty on the inside and who they could truly be,
Through the eyes of a child, not knowing this Earth,
Excitable yet uneducated, of the horrors of death and birth.

Clara Hayward (12)
The Hammond School, Chester

Through Her Eyes

As I wonder how she wakes up so perfectly,
I decide to look through her eyes, not knowing how wrong I could be.
She's sat in the mirror crying with tears,
Asking herself why she has no peers.
She starts to get ready, doing her make-up
She's pretty without it, how could she cover that up?
She walks to her wardrobe to pick out an outfit.
She wonders if she needs an Instagram filter
Or if she would be fine without it.

I was happier as a kid
Why not now?
She starts to frown until she hears a loud bang
And turns around,
"Get your breakfast now!"
She stands still for a minute or so
Debating whether to go
"I'll have it later," she said
Oh no, I knew she wouldn't get it
She never did
She thinks it doesn't matter but yes it does.

Felicity Gray-Shaw (12)
The Hammond School, Chester

Teen Life

She wakes up, looks at her phone,
Does her make-up, has a moan,
She doesn't feel she's as pretty as everyone else,
She doesn't think she's needed here.

She skips most meals, but nothing ever changes,
It makes her feel worse, nothing the same.
She thinks back to when she was a little girl,
Careless and free, she thought she could do anything,
In this cruel world, like drink a tea or eat a pea.

"She's just dramatic," "Always complaining,"
But they don't understand, they don't see her at night,
Crying head in hand.

Her mask is gone, hair frizzled and frazzled,
But she can't stop now, she's in too deep,
It's the only task she'll always complete.

Harriet Maughan (12)
The Hammond School, Chester

Toxic Eyes

As I see through her eyes,
She sits there in sadness in her pearl-filled world,
The gold and glamour is just a cover to things that happen,
Beyond the gate, and beyond the door,
The Bentley outside and the Ferrari in the drive,
From her rich boyfriend who she loves,
But behind all of that she is just a girl,
Who is scared for herself,
Her boyfriend comes home, not sober at all,
With anger in his eyes.

He seems annoyed, and she is paranoid,
Like most nights when he comes home,
She weeps and she cries, out of her eyes,
What has he done, should not have drunk rum,
The police are here and she's going,
Who knows where the spark she had goes,
After the murder is done.

Christie Morgan (12)
The Hammond School, Chester

Influencers

Imagine yourself as an influencer.
Imagine how many people there would be counting on you.
So much hate on all of your accounts,
And sleepless nights thinking of ideas,
To get more followers and drown out the hate.

But instead of ideas filling your head,
The hate that was built up over the years,
The stalkers that follow you around the streets,
Fill your head with horrible, horrible thoughts.

But against all this bad, there is some light,
A light that drowns out most of the dark.
Subscribers, followers and fans
Are the ones that give you hope again.
You can change the world by talking about something.
So pick up a camera and start walking.

Catherine Hampson (12)
The Hammond School, Chester

Untitled

The pain of knowing,
Watching his energy slowing.
You never realise how precious time is,
Until you start to lose it.
Knowing his pain,
Knowing life would never be the same.

Seeing the symptoms,
Knowing the victims.
Cancer is a killer,
Makes you look in the mirror,
And think, *could this happen to me?*

I just wish people would see,
This isn't something to joke about,
Or something to make you smile.

It could be your nan,
This is more than,
What you see on TV,
This is reality.

1,000 a day,
Hear a doctor say,
"It's cancer,"
What about the girl
Who wanted to be a dancer?

Too busy with hospital visits,
Too busy to follow her dreams.
Surrounded by machines,
Her body pushed to extremes.

Everyone telling her, "You'll be okay,"
But who are they to say?
She just wants to play with her friend,
When will this end?

But there is that fifty percent,
Who get to ring that bell,
And start to feel well,
But only time can tell.

Bethany Pearson (13)
Trinity High School, Redditch

I've Only Ever Wanted To Look Like You

As I look through the mirror, here emerges my reflection,
No matter how I look, there is no sight of perfection.
I only want to look away, but my head is still as a statue,
I've only ever wanted to look like you.

As waterfalls pour from my eyes,
I can only think of ones that look like diamonds in the skies,
My eyes are an ugly brown,
I might as well be a circus clown.

The shape of my nose is crooked and disfigured,
While other ones are perfect and glow,
While I sit here and look like a crow,
Is there any way to fix it?

My teeth are crooked and yellow,
It hurts just to open my mouth and say hello,
Others are perfect and angelic white,
Improving mine is nowhere in sight.

I can't stop being fixated on how others look like moths to a flame,
I can only exist and live in shame,
I wish I could just be different and look brand new,
I've only ever wanted to look like you.

Kaiden Collins-Evans (13)
Trinity High School, Redditch

An Actor's View

I love that feeling
you know that feeling
when the seams of my costume touch
my nervous skin.
When 'Act One Beginners' is projected
in my dressing room
That pure sound of excited chat from the audience as they take their seats,
the very seats they'll leave in two hours' time
a changed person.

I can't get over that feeling.
Where your whole body tingles from stepping on stage for the first time.
Only then does my character begin
I am no longer me, I am them.
It's like a soul of life stepping into my very shoes.
This story on stage is real.
And when the audience has clapped
and the curtain has fallen, I'll turn to my cast mate and we will both say,
"See you at the stage door tomorrow."
Because the story remains on that
wooden stage
ready to be picked up for a whole new
audience tomorrow.
And that's the beauty of theatre.

Oliver Cureton-Phillips (14)
Trinity High School, Redditch

Perfect?

Perfect?
Sometimes I wish I could lend you my eyes,
lend you my hips,
lend you my thighs.
Sometimes I wish I could take a new shape,
look how I want without feeling so fake.
Lucky is he, who lives unaware, doesn't get bothered by those who don't care,
Lucky is he, who lives unaware, doesn't get bothered by all that's unfair,
Unlucky me, who knows way too much.
Tries to fit in, but fails at such.
...Sometimes I wish you could see what I see,
the same reflection, I hate seeing in front of me.
But at the same time, I'd hate you to see me that way,
a pile of atrocities, given a name.
The scars on my limbs, I wish to fade.
But nothing, nothing, will make me feel the same.
Sometimes the truth is just my point of view,
not what is real,
not what is true.

Ashton Hands (13)
Trinity High School, Redditch

Flipped

My life will always be the same,
waking up at 6am in the morning,
to the sound of the busy town,
wondering what I will do today.
I take the same route to work,
down that same narrow lane,
I pass the very bus stop,
where I used to wait every day,
I get through the lengthy day at work,
that seems to go on for hours.
I get home and go to bed,
I wake up the next morning,
expecting my life to be the very same.
That was until it wasn't...

Our cars collided with one another,
the impact so shocking,
I thought it was all over.
I was lucky enough to be so fortunate,
I think we should all do more with life,
as we never know what may happen.
I thought my life would always be the same,
until it wasn't.
Now my life is flipped.

Evie Hawkins (14)
Trinity High School, Redditch

The Starlings

What a time it was to be alive
Just for a moment, I felt free.

I let go of me,
No one captured what I saw, the calling of the sky
...them, an echo through my head.
no one captured what I did, the sensation of nature.

Every beat, recalling every stroke of that brush, that painted that sky.
Directing my eye,
Mesmerising the skies,
Just for a moment. I felt free,
Felt the guidence they connected to me,
The loving sense of belonging.

The breeze of life that boosts my soul,
Freer than time that doesn't age,
Freer than a cheetah out of its cage,
Every second ticked another twist of hope,
Unlocked from all burdens.

An unforgettable moment...
An inevitable sight...

We are the Starlings.

Falak Aziz (14)
Trinity High School, Redditch

Red And Blue

Your top is red,
My top is blue,
Does that make me any different than you?
The fabric is woven all the same way,
Mine's frayed at the edges,
Still to see another day,
Yours is stretched at the collar,
Through wear and through tear,
So just take a minute to stop and compare,
Is my top any different to yours,
Should it change who I am,
My employment, housing and life?
If I'm stuck in poverty, who can be my wife?
The answer is no, and plainly that,
So if my skin is black and yours is white,
Does that change the equation,
Of red and blue tops?
Of who gets their masters and who calls the shots,
My life is in danger,
Though it shouldn't be,
Organs keep me alive, why is this endangering me?

Millie Jones (13)
Trinity High School, Redditch

Unrivaled

Life and death, ambition and exploration, all themes for the
one true goal of any samurai-
being 'Unrivaled under the heavens'.
Nurture is the source.
Tales and legends being told,
expecting these events in their own lives to unfold.

Growing up, strength is the objective,
but once the quest begins there is more to be contemplated.
Takezo understands this - the truth of introspection.
How the path isn't linear and requires correct perception.

He adds nuance to his quest
and knows not to immediately strive to be the best,
and follow the rest.
But what happens is different from what he expected,
his experiences were solely asserted on wisdom.

Ayaan Hussain (14)
Trinity High School, Redditch

Who They Are

When they walk through the streets and halls,
Other sets of eyes darting to walls,
Their confidence and pride in who they are falls.
Just because of who they are.

People steering clear,
Society making them believe they should fear,
Just because of their actions and looks,
Which isn't written in the books.
Just because of who they are.

Not wanting to be in this world anymore,
Their personality broken and torn,
Leaving the people that really care to mourn.

They say it's not natural,
Just because they aren't as perfect or as straight as an equilateral.
Just because of who they are.

Izzy Louth (14)
Trinity High School, Redditch

2022 Summer, Like No Other

Have you ever cycled so far into the countryside, it felt like another country?
Have you ever built a den and then almost burnt it down?
Have you ever swung so high above a ditch you felt like Superman?
Have you ever jumped in a river without knowing where it ends?
Have you ever had a football match where the losers get egged?
Have you ever felt so much joy you felt like school would never start again?
Have you ever had so many crashes, bumps, fights that you felt numb?

Will anyone ever accomplish what we did that summer?
Have you ever felt on top of the world for six weeks
Like we did?

Kye McEntee (13)
Trinity High School, Redditch

The People Marched

As I looked,
The people marched,
And they yelled,
"Death to the government,"
As I watched,
The police marched on them,
And I saw,
The police went down,
And as I watched,
The looters burned and stole,
And in came the army,
And the army went down,
As I watched,
The people burned 10 Downing Street,
As I watched,
The government burned,
And then they marched,
On Buckingham Palace,
And empty and desolate,
The heart of our country burned,
And then the people yelled,
"Death to the government!"

Henry Power (13)
Trinity High School, Redditch

Capturing The Moment

The camera takes the shot,
Capturing the moment from the hot summer day,
The cameraman captures the moment,
The glass lens works with the camera,
Capturing the moment.

The sunset is full of character in the photo,
Capturing the moment,
The noise distracted the cameraman from capturing the moment,
The hands of the cameraman remain still,
Capturing the moment.

The camera could break,
Not capturing the moment,
The cameraman's fingers slip,
Not capturing the moment,
The camera has a crack,
Not capturing the moment.

William Bussey (14)
Trinity High School, Redditch

The Dark, Deep Ocean

The ocean is dark
It's hidden away
People are scared
The ocean is big and a mystery.
The ocean can cause emotion
For those from war,
Lost at sea and
Portrays the image of their past.

Some dwell on the past
Despite therapy,
Some hide their pain
By saying they're fine.
The ocean deep, dark, cold,
Big, beautiful.
People like the ocean,
People hate the ocean
People are scared
Because only five percent of the ocean,
Has been explored.
So it's really a mystery.

Cameron Lewis (13)
Trinity High School, Redditch

Old-Fashioned Fun

Getting ready for the day,
Stepping in the car,
You're on your way.

Walking up with your mates,
You have talked about this,
On different dates.

Throwing the ball down the alley,
Having lots of fun,
Enjoying yourself,
Not wanting this to ever be done.

Losing track of time,
Laughing with your friends,
Without realising,
This is coming to an end.

Going home,
After everyone is done,
Then you think to yourself,
Is there anything more fun?

George Coates (14)
Trinity High School, Redditch

Teenage Years

In the whirlwind of teenage years I stand,
A kaleidoscope of dreams at my command,
With laughter ringing and tears that flow,
I try to make the most of this journey, highs and lows.

I don't quite know where I'm going in this life,
The future cannot be told,
I'm constantly changing what I want to become when I grow old.
So here I stand, in this teenage space
With dreams to chase and fears to face.

I am the author of my own story,
A teenage girl in all her glory.

Mia Barwick (14)
Trinity High School, Redditch

Clouds

Clouds are like people,
people are like clouds,
clouds are all different,
different but unique,
unique just like people,
people are like clouds,
different shapes and sizes,
all beautiful in their own way,
no need to change it,
clouds are like people,
people are like clouds,
everybody should be accepted,
no matter how they look,
clouds are like people,
people are like clouds.

Molly Byrne-Smith (14)
Trinity High School, Redditch

Paradise

Looking through the splashed goggles on my face,
I see the sun resting on top of the ocean.
Yellow, blue, purple, pink,
All of those colours I see in front of me, take over the moment.
Dolphins splash over each other,
And into the water
I go under and see a beautiful sight,
Light is shining in all directions,
Reflecting off coral and bringing happiness to life.
What an amazing sight.

Elsie Kalaker (14)
Trinity High School, Redditch

YOUNG WRITERS INFORMATION

We hope you have enjoyed reading this book – and that you will continue to in the coming years.

If you're a young writer who enjoys reading and creative writing, or the parent of an enthusiastic poet or story writer, do visit our website **www.youngwriters.co.uk**. Here you will find free competitions, workshops and games, as well as recommended reads, a poetry glossary and our blog. There's lots to keep budding writers motivated to write!

If you would like to order further copies of this book, or any of our other titles, then please give us a call or order via your online account.

Young Writers
Remus House
Coltsfoot Drive
Peterborough
PE2 9BF
(01733) 890066
info@youngwriters.co.uk

Join in the conversation!
Tips, news, giveaways and much more!

YoungWritersUK   YoungWritersCW
youngwriterscw   youngwriterscw